THE ANSWER
IS
IN YOUR HANDS

BE ABOUT SUCCESS!

Believe + Achieve!

Transcendent Minds Press

The Answer is in Your Hands: Be About Success! Dr. Derek Greenfield

ISBN 978-0-9797294-0-9

Cover design and photography by Derek Greenfield

Dedicated to my family, my friends, my students... and to all those who struggle to beat the odds, who fight for equality, and who never give up on their dreams.

"Service to others is the rent we pay for living."
-Marian Wright Edelman

"There is no progress without struggle."
-Frederick Douglass

"If you're going to do something, do it right!"
-Jerry Greenfield (my dad)

TABLE OF CONTENTS

ACKNOWLEDGEMENTS

It is my good fortune in life to have been raised in a wonderful and loving family, to have been taught by outstanding educators, to have worked with some incredibly talented colleagues and students, and to have made friends with dynamic people across the globe. While I have certainly faced my fair share of challenges (as I will discuss in this book), I know that the encouragement and wisdom of so many individuals has sustained and guided me through these experiences. In many ways, this book is intended to represent a gesture of appreciation for their efforts.

In particular, I must give praise to my parents, Jerry and Maxene Greenfield, for their unwavering support and the positive example they have always set. Jeff and Johanna, my oldest brother and sister-in-law, are loving individuals who remain committed to healthy living and social justice. My brother David and his wife Sue have always made me feel welcome in their family and also serve as model parents. With my recent move to North Carolina, I have been able to enjoy spending considerable time with my niece Lindsay and nephew Mark, and I find myself so impressed by their talents and sensitivity to others.

I am thankful for my closest friends - Roxanne Peyton, Xavier Esters, Darryl Brice, Mike Titlebaum, Bryan Elliott, Angela Caraway, Stacy Walden, LaShawn Morgan, and Jason Oliver – for being there when I needed to talk, for making life even more fun, and for doing the great work they do. The following list of former teachers, colleagues, and students includes individuals who have inspired and mentored me in a variety of ways: Aaron Reader; Valerie Burgest; Yoshiko Harden; Bruce Roberts; Dr. Jack Bermingham; Jeff Wagnitz; Dr. Jean Harris; Dawn Henderson; Dr. Paul Bernstein; Dr. Bob Baugher; Dr. Aldon Morris; Dr. Maria Febbo-Hunt; Brandon Reed; Tiayea Culbreath; Davis Northern; Douglas Curry; Ismael Seals; Tasha Williams; Rodney Lindsey; Dr. Leslie Frost; Dr. Hellenna Terrell; Desiree Urquhart; Kareem Levi; Graylin Bateast; Darrick Brown; Natasha Burrowes; Christopher Jones; Heather Drake; Dr. Jocelyn Taliaferro; Dr. Jessica Decuir-Gunby; Dr. James Seymour; Dr. Norris Gunby; Dr. Grant Holley; Dr. Michael Maher; Hope Quallo; Dr. Stanley Elliott; Sarah Winston; Michael Walton; Tavar Proctor; Brian McClelland; Dr. Charles Payne; Dr. Rajendra Chetty; Dr. James Banks; Abeni El-Amin; Mary Ann Satter; J. Allan Tyler; Donald Summons; Landon Adams; Joe Gattis; and Dr. Bob Hughes. My apologies for not being able to mention the names of all the countless others who have made a valuable impact on my life.

This book has been a true labor of love, and I've enjoyed the opportunity to assemble these thoughts to offer to readers. I hope that I have sufficiently honored all those whose presence has benefited my life with the words that follow – and that you find the stories, ideas, and experiences that I share to be rewarding sources of insight and inspiration. I take full responsibility for the words written in these pages and welcome any concerns, compliments, criticisms, or comments via e-mail at derek@derekgreenfield.com.

INTRODUCTION

The Answer is in Your Hands: Be About Success!

I recall my first major engagement as a motivational speaker about fifteen years ago, when I was invited to deliver a presentation in front of 500 ninth graders during an orientation assembly. While I felt a bit nervous about this exciting opportunity, I was well prepared and started out strong. My spirit soared with the successful use of every creative activity and example. With about five minutes remaining, a student in the front row raised his hand; I figured that he would offer some meaningful comment or perhaps even words of praise. To ensure that everyone would hear, the young man proceeded to shout out, "Hey man, your zipper is down!" You can imagine how an auditorium full of ninth graders responded – with those last few moments seeming like a painful eternity. With insufficient experience and little confidence, I didn't quite know how to handle the situation or the boisterous crowd. As a result of the chaotic scene that ensued, the principal later informed me, "You'll never be asked back here again."

Consumed by embarrassment, I drove home in a state of disappointment and started questioning whether I would ever want to take another risk to speak to a big group. Perhaps the whole ordeal signaled that I was not meant to do this kind of work. I began to doubt myself, my abilities, and my goals.

But then, I recalled a few examples that I shared with those students about facing adversity with courage and dedication.

One of the most important traits we can possess is resilience. As I had informed them, Dr. Seuss' first book was rejected by twenty-seven different publishers. Rather than becoming discouraged and abandoning the dream, he continued to fine-tune the book until someone finally believed in its merits. Michael Jordan was cut from his first high school basketball team. To think what would have happened if, like many of us, they had given up after encountering a single setback!

Since I encouraged others to persevere in the midst of resistance, I had to practice what I preached. Indeed, life is ten percent what happens to you, and ninety percent how you respond! We have to be willing to handle challenges with dignity and determination in order to prevent ourselves from giving in to passivity and pessimism. While we're bound to face obstacles and opposition, it is within us to generate the strength and courage needed to keep on keepin' on. After all, a diamond is just a lump of coal with persistence.

Interestingly enough, the Japanese word for crisis involves two distinct symbolic characters. One denotes danger — and it's clear that any crisis situation could lead to serious problems. However, the other character means opportunity. All apparent crises give us opportunities to come up with new and better solutions.

As famed author Iyanla Vanzant proclaims, negative moments in our lives can actually be seen as blessings, because they provide us with possibilities for gaining insights and motivation that benefit us in the long run. Consider a time in your life when you endured something painful. Maybe it was a bad romantic relationship, the death of a close family member, or a failed opportunity to get ahead. Sure, it hurt... but if you're honest with yourself, you'll probably acknowledge that it ended up being an incredibly valuable learning experience. Maybe now you know better about how to handle disappointment. Maybe you discovered the importance of living life to the fullest. Maybe you were finally able to let go of a toxic person with whom you shared a miserable relationship. When I ask audience members during my presentations to raise their hands if these traumatic moments were ultimately a "good thing," the response is almost unanimous. Indeed, according to the late John H. Johnson, founder of Johnson Publishing Company, "We learn from failure much more than from success."

Painful encounters can either drive you crazy... or be used to drive you to greatness. I'd prefer to maintain control of my own life and utilize these moments to motivate me to something higher and better. Again, it's not easy, but it's possible. I can certainly understand how someone who has experienced trauma and tragedy could become brokenhearted or cynical, but I don't understand why he or she would want to stay in that mental prison and not at least fight back. I remember using an odd example years ago with a gang member who continuously remained passive when dealing with life's emotional challenges. When I asked him what he would do if someone walked up and slapped him across the face, he brazenly asserted that he would be ready to fight. Then, I asked him why he didn't fight back when life seemed to keep slapping him across the face. He had no verbal response, but he saw my point. We can and must believe that we deserve the best and be willing to put in the work to keep ourselves on track even when outside forces attempt to derail us.

I know for certain that the process of handling some difficult experiences has made me a better person. Back in my 20s, I went through an agonizing few months that brought me down emotionally. I was struggling to find myself or my direction in life, but fortunately, I had people to talk to for support and guidance. Not only did this painful period force me to ultimately make some critical discoveries about myself, but I gained greater empathy and understanding of others who were enduring life struggles. It was tough stuff, but I'm glad it happened. Indeed, we can crash and burn – or choose to crash and learn. As Dr. King proclaimed, "Only when it is dark enough can you see the stars."

Perhaps the story of Lance Armstrong can serve as the perfect example of how negatives can truly become positives. Way back in 1996, Lance was diagnosed with testicular cancer that had actually metastasized to his brain and lungs. Keep in mind that he had yet to become a superstar cyclist by that time. But, spurred on by the challenge of conquering the disease, Lance developed a workout regiment and a determined focus that ultimately led him to win seven straight Tour de France events. If he had not been subjected to this incredible hardship, it is possible that he would never have become such a dominant champion. As Lance once stated, "Each time I encountered suffering, I believe that I grew, and further defined my capacities

— not just my physical ones, but my interior ones as well, for contentment, friendship, or any other human experience." Going through pain allows us to more fully appreciate our accomplishments and truly feel the joy of success.

So, as you travel through life, I encourage you to hold these ideas in your mind and heart. If something doesn't work the first time, don't give up - evaluate the situation and identify a better strategy for success. Simply put, stay positive, find ways to benefit, and keep advancing. As for me, I request a podium wherever I speak, so that I can always sneak behind it temporarily and check the zipper to ensure that it has not betrayed me again! Again, life is ten percent what happens to us, and ninety percent how we respond.

I'd like to share a fictional tale about two mischievous teenage boys who decided to play a trick on an old wise woman living on the top of a nearby hill. Rumor had it that no one had ever been able to stump the woman with an intellectual riddle, but these boys were determined to make their mark. The plan was to place a small bird in the hands of the first boy, with the second boy asking the woman if the bird were alive or dead. If she responded that the bird was alive, the first boy would immediately compress his hands, killing the helpless creature. But if the woman stated that the bird was dead, the hands would open and the bird would fly away into freedom. Either way, the boys were convinced that they would trick her.

That evening, following hours of difficult hiking, the boys located the isolated shack of the wise elder. Full of excitement, they burst into her home and gleefully proclaimed, "We have the one riddle you will never be able to answer!" The old woman paused, and then nodded her head once, indicating her readiness for the challenge. The second boy sped through his opening statement: "OK, here's an easy one for you. What does my friend have in his hands?" Before even hearing the end of the question, the woman told them they were in possession of a bird. The same boy arrogantly responded, "Yeah, that's true. But... is the bird alive or dead?"

The woman's eyes glazed over, her right hand wiping a bead of sweat from her wrinkled forehead. When she started looking out the window, the boys giggled like toddlers playing their first game of peek-a-boo. Suddenly, she began to smile. Looking down on the boys, the old woman regained the throne: "Young men, I have the answer for you. The answer... is in your hands!"

Just like the fate of the bird, our destiny rests in our hands as well. We possess the power to control our lives. No matter what cards we are dealt, we can turn the hand into a winner. It does us no good to relinquish control to others or blame external factors for our shortcomings - as we won't be granted any sympathy points when applying for a job. Furthermore, regardless of our age, background, financial status, or any other characteristic, we have the potential to go beyond what might be considered possible for us. I have heard many stories of incredible young people who are changing the world as well as 90-year-olds who fulfill a childhood dream of college graduation. I've worked with students who remained committed to success even as their own parents tried to destroy their spirit. At my college, a blind student currently holds the top grade in his Statistics course. It's up to us to seize the reins in life, and this book is designed to assist you in empowering yourself with the attitudes and skills needed for achieving your goals.

Here's a quick activity for you: Reach your hands into the air as high as you possibly can. (Actually do this now, and I'll wait for you.)

Hold this position for a few seconds.

Now, reach higher.

(OK, once you've done that, you can put your tired arms down.)

Did you notice that you reached higher the second time, even though I asked you to reach *as high as you possibly could* the first time? Think about it – while we may often feel that we are producing our best, we have the capability for even greater effort and performance. So, the next time you claim that you're giving all you can, remember this mini-exercise and dig down deeper to find that extra energy to do more and to do better. In the words of famed educator Benjamin Mays, "Low aim, not failure, is sin." We can always transcend our perceived limitations, and by setting higher expectations for ourselves, we end up accomplishing so much more in life. When you shoot for the moon, even if you come up a little bit short, you still end up with a whole bunch of stars.

I enjoy reading powerful quotations, as they can capture profound ideas in a concise way. Here are a few for you:

"Even if you are on the right track, you'll get run over if you just sit there!"
—*Will Rogers*

"It matters not the number of years in your life. It is the life in your years."
—*Abraham Lincoln*

"Remember, no one can make you feel inferior without your consent."
—*Eleanor Roosevelt*

"Some people give gifts that fit on mantles, while others give gifts of positive examples."
—*KRS-One*

"The point is not to pay back kindness, but to pass it on."
—*Julia Alvarez*

"Be yourself. An original is always worth more than a copy."
—*Unknown*

"You say this is a computer for ordinary people? Why would an ordinary person want a computer?"
—*Hewlett Packard executive to Steve Wozniak regarding Apple prototype*

Finally, I'm reminded of a story of a 3rd grade girl who sat at her desk working intently on a drawing. Her teacher walked by to ask about the main character in the picture, and the girl proudly responded that she was drawing God. Taken aback by the comment, the teacher proceeded to state, "I'm sorry, sweetie, but no one knows what God looks like." Without hesitation, the girl replied, "They will, in a minute." Imagine now if we all operated with the same certainty that, despite what others may think or regardless of what's come before us, we can make the seemingly impossible *possible*.

I have divided the main ideas of this book into five chapters, each one corresponding to a theme of importance. The letters of the acronym ABOUT stand for a series of concepts that I believe must be addressed in order for us to maximize our potential and create a better world overall. We need to be ABOUT the business of success. We must endeavor to learn ABOUT ourselves and others. And we benefit from getting out and ABOUT to actively pursue our dreams with purpose and passion. Hopefully, you'll find this book to be a helpful companion in your life journey.

Let's get started!
First fill-in-the-blank: I am reading this book because:

_____

_____

_____

_____

_____

_____

_____

_____

_____

_____

_____

_____

Things I learned or thought about when reading this chapter:

_____

_____

_____

_____

_____

_____

_____

_____

_____

_____

_____

_____

_____

ATTITUDE
ATTITUDES ARE CONTAGIOUS... MAKE YOURS WORTH CATCHING!

As Henry Ford asserted, "If you think you can do a thing or that you cannot do a thing, in either case you are right." It seems obvious that how we feel about ourselves and about life will profoundly impact our ability to accomplish our goals. You have to be convinced that your dreams are possible and to be willing to take the chance to make them happen. Now, if you doubt that your attitude really is everything in life, check this out. Assign points to each letter in the word "attitude" based on its place in the alphabet. For example, "a" gets one point (the first letter in the alphabet) and "t" would receive twenty points (twentieth letter). Once you finish with all the eight letters in the word, count up the points and then continue reading.

If your math is correct, you'll find the sum to be 100. Yes, attitude is 100% of what's needed to fulfill our promise in life!

To quote an old saying, "Your attitude determines your altitude" - as your ability to soar high in life correlates with your state of mind. Continuing with this flight metaphor, scientists will confirm the fact that, due to its huge body and tiny wings, the bumble bee should not be capable of flying. Well, Mother Nature must have forgotten to tell the bumblebee - and the bumblebee flies because it knows that it can.

I remember meeting a young woman who was seriously injured

in a car crash and subsequently told she'd never walk again. Yet, by listening to her heart and believing in herself, she proved the doctors wrong. People look surprised when I walk into a room to conduct a session on hip-hop culture, but after dropping my rhymes on them, their view changes. We cannot allow others' negativity or narrow perspective of the world to divert us from our destiny. Albert Einstein was considered slow as a child, and we know what happened.

If we intend to live a meaningful, productive life in which we actively pursue and accomplish our goals, we have to know that we are worthy and capable. The stories from the Introduction remind us that we're going to face challenges and even disappointments, but we must remain upbeat and strong in the mission to experience success. I just believe that it takes a healthy dose of PMA – positive mental attitude!

As the title of this chapter states, attitudes are contagious. At some point, you've probably worked at a job or been part of a social group in which one individual's negative attitude began to infect everyone. I remember consulting with a department in which the constant bickering of two people completely drained their co-workers of energy, inevitably making the office an extremely uncomfortable place for everyone. On the other hand, I was fortunate enough to once have a colleague whose positive energy (and frequent rounds to our offices with candy) kept everyone's spirits high. One person's attitude can make or break a situation.

The contagion of attitudes spreads throughout our soul and also influences the kinds of people we attract. Once people become committed to negative thinking, their entire way of being is infected – and they typically seek out other miserable people to confirm the validity of their outlook. As the saying goes, "misery loves company." Conversely, healthy people want to be surrounded by others who bring positive energy and motivate them for greatness. Since "birds of a feather flock together," take a peek at your flock.

So, what attitude do you bring to life? Right now, think about your possible reputation among others. When you walk in a room, are they gladly expressing, "Hey, look who's here!" or painfully saying under their breath, "Oh darn, look who's here?" Do you help bring out the best in others? What example do you set? Are you a constant complainer or a magical motivator?

Some readers might be wondering how they can remain positive when immersed in negative environments. The Noah Principle proclaims, "There are no prizes for predicting rain – only rewards for building arks." It is meaningless to just complain or explain what's wrong, unless you are willing to make something better happen. Simply put, if you are not part of the solution, YOU are part of the problem! Even by just staying out of the way, you're consenting to the situation and allowing the same conditions to persist. Isn't there something that you could do to generate a little improvement?

Take your index finger and pretend to point it at someone (symbolizing that you're blaming them). I hope that you notice how three of the other fingers are curled in such a way as to point directly back at you! Instead of merely blaming others, see your role in the dilemma and determine what you can do about it. Hopefully, this little example can illustrate the importance of looking at yourself to decide how you can take control of your life and work towards making the best of any situation.

Developing and continuously carrying a good attitude around with us enhances the possibility of success. People want to support others who are enthusiastic and inspiring, and this positive spirit propels us to be driven to accept greater challenges. Even my uncommon answer to the routine question, "How are you?" surprises folks. Rather than the typical "Fine" (or even "I'm living... surviving... hanging in there"... or as a colleague of mine once said, "I'm upright and taking nourishment"), I respond with extra emphasis, "Terrific and getting better!" When you think positively, more positive things are likely to happen around you. It takes 70 muscles to frown and only 14 muscles to smile, so I refuse to work five times harder to be miserable!

I recently challenged one of the members of our school's tennis team to some friendly competition. In the midst of being beaten quite soundly, I rolled my ankle and experienced tremendous pain. While I probably ought to have called it a day, I felt the urge to at least see how I would perform. It didn't go well – yet I didn't want to give up. Then, as I seriously considered the notion of quitting, I hit a great shot for a winner. And then another. Literally, as the adrenaline kicked in and my confidence swelled, I took charge of the match and proceeded to grab the victory. My spirit wouldn't allow me to lose, and indeed, it was yet another case of mind and soul over matter.

On the following page, you'll see a diagram. Take a brief look at it now and then move on to the next page.

Paris
in the
the Spring

Based on your memory, how many words did you see printed inside the triangle? (Think of your answer before continuing to read.)

Most people notice four words: Paris in the Spring. However, if you check out the page again, you will discover that, in actuality, five words are present. How can that be? This exercise offers a critical lesson about the power of the mind. Since your brain doesn't expect to see "Paris in the the Spring," it blocks out the second "the" so that the sentence makes sense. While in some ways it's nice that you possess this grammatical correction censor, it's also clear you weren't even aware that your brain erased the word. Indeed, sometimes we may not realize how our mind might be similarly "blocking out" other relevant and beneficial information, based on the fact that it doesn't anticipate encountering those ideas.

I have met so many people who don't expect to do well and literally believe that they are not worthy of good things. As a result, they don't allow themselves to "see" the positive opportunities and experiences right in front of their noses. Since they tune out those chances and avoid good fortune, they end up remaining precisely where they are in life. It's generally not an issue of talent or intrinsic desire – it's just their brain holding onto negative images and filtering out the good.

Thus, we can actually be our own worst enemy. Have *you* ever talked yourself out of going for something you really desired? Research has shown that about 87% of our self-talk is negative; now imagine what we could accomplish if we believed in ourselves and acted with conviction that we were obligated to strive for excellence! By training our brains to think positively, we can unleash tremendous potential.

Check this out: "The phemnnoeal pweor of the hmuan mnid."

Aoccdrnig to rscheearch at Cmabrigde Uinervtisy, it deosn't mttaer in waht oredr the ltteers in a wrod are, the olny iprmoetnt tihng is taht the frist and lsat ltteer be at the rghit pclae. The rset can be a total mses and you can sitll raed it wouthit a porbelm. Tihs is bcuseae the huamn mnid deos not raed ervey lteter by istlef, but the wrod as a wlohe.

Amzanig, huh?

The brain is a pretty incredible instrument! And just like any muscle in the body, it can be strengthened. As Jeff Howard, founder of The Efficacy Institute, asserts, "Smart is not something you are. Smart is something you get." Through hard work, we can improve our intelligence and our positive mindset.

Language is a powerful fuel source for improving the functioning of this main engine, our brain. A concept called the Sapir–Whorf Hypothesis suggests that language structures reality – in other words, the way we talk shapes how we think and behave. For example, social service providers no longer refer to an individual experiencing sexual assault as a "victim." Instead, the word "survivor" is used, granting more autonomy to the individual in the recovery process. A victim is a person who something happens to – survivors take charge of their lives.

I recall reading a story about a scientist who noticed that no members of the nomadic tribe he studied ever stuttered. After inquiring about the situation, he found out that no word for stutter even existed in their vocabulary. In many cases, if we don't know about it, we don't do it. Imagine if we didn't even consider the word "failure" and only thought about "perseverance" or "success," we would automatically keep going with confidence. We'd just know that we had to get it done.

Similarly, the highly successful former football coach Jimmy Johnson never told his running backs "don't fumble" since that command places the notion of fumbling central in the player's mind. Thinking about fumbling increases the likelihood of doing it. Instead, he instructed them to "hold onto the ball," something that accentuated their goal in a more positive manner. What we say affects what we think – which ultimately impacts what we do. We can all benefit from paying closer attention to the words emanating from our mouths and how they shape our life outcomes.

A short time ago, I was introduced to an idea in consulting referred to as "appreciative inquiry." Its basic premise is that we get in life what we focus on, and as a result, organizations are more likely to progress when identifying collective strengths and building upon them rather than focusing solely on weaknesses. We tend not to grow as much when being reminded of our shortcomings. Making more "good stuff" tends to produce greater benefits than attempting to eliminate "bad stuff."

When students in one of my classes were constantly complaining about the problems at our school, I proceeded to facilitate a discussion of all the positive elements of the institution. Immediately, they started to realize how many wonderful things they had been taking for granted. Now, I'm not advocating ignoring the problems – just that we're more likely to erase them when replacing them with strengths. Before, it was a common refrain to hear students despondently proclaim "That's our school" whenever something went wrong. In the end, that line reinforced a negative, passive attitude that just assumed the inevitability of failure and inhibited any motivation to seek a change. But after making our positive list, it was amazing to hear those same students have fun by, for example, pointing to a great professor and saying to each other with pride, "That's our school!" It's not just an exercise in niceness — the activity actually produces tangible change. Do it sometime and see what happens.

This concept represents the reason why I become so frustrated when I hear adults discuss the notion of "at risk" youth. In my view, the label automatically presumes that the child is a potential problem that must be prevented instead of a wonderful and talented young person who just needs direction to bring forth all his gifts. This focus on supposed pathology ignores the considerable potential waiting to be identified and nurtured. Keeping someone from doing bad is nowhere near as successful as promoting positivity. It does no good to try to get a teenager to avoid pregnancy if she has no plan for her future. When we help her to recognize her skills and to begin developing an agenda for success, she automatically becomes less likely to engage in risky behavior. Thus, I prefer to consider these young people as "at-success," believing that they are all on the verge of greatness.

Years ago, psychologists Robert Rosenthal and Leonore Jacobson conducted a study in which they administered an IQ test to first-grade classes at the beginning of the school year. After tabulating the results, the researchers proceeded to inform the teachers that twenty percent of the children had performed in such a way that they had been identified as "bloomers," or students predicted to experience a tremendous intellectual spurt during the year. Subsequent testing at the end of the school year revealed that these "bloomers" increased their IQs by 27.4 points, far exceeding the "regular" students whose growth only averaged 11 points. Yet, the key issue is that no real concept of "bloomers" existed, as the students in this category were randomly selected and not any more advanced than the others. With the positive labels, the teachers started challenging and encouraging the "bloomers" more, and through a clear case of self-fulfilling prophecy, spurred them to greater intellectual development. Can you imagine what would happen if teachers similarly believed in the potential of all young people!

So, how do all these ideas apply to you personally? I'll ask you to think about some aspect of your life that you tend to see in a negative light or find yourself complaining about a great deal. What words do you use when discussing this situation? How do you communicate these feelings to others? Why do you respond this way? Now, let's work together to envision ways to use language and perception for more positive purposes. How could you alter the manner in which you speak about the issue to reduce the negativity – as indeed, is it possible that your words could be making the situation even worse? Is there any good side to all of this? What could you possibly gain by adjusting what you say (or maybe just by cutting back on the incredible amount of time and energy wasted by moaning about it)?

Take some time to process these questions.

Building from this idea of the power of language, I'd like to challenge readers to remove "Five Dirty Words" from their vocabularies. Why would a college professor seek to weaken our knowledge base? In my opinion, some words actually function to reduce productivity, and we'd benefit from avoiding their use in most cases. First, let's look at the word "BUT." "But it can't be done," "But it's not possible," "But it's not my job," "But we don't have the budget," "But I'm not capable of doing it," and "But what if it doesn't work?" The word inherently creates a roadblock for effort and performance. By showing our BUTS, we accept failure and minimize growth opportunities. Our society needs to have "emotional weight-loss centers" on every corner because we have some awfully big BUTS! If we would only get our BUTS out of the way, we could accomplish a great deal more.

The second deadly word is "TRY." You might be tempted to ask, what could be so bad about trying, since it seems better than not even bothering, right? Well, remember the last time you said that you would "try" to do something. Maybe it was the decision to "try" to clean the garage, or perhaps you stated that you would "try" to stay in touch with a new acquaintance from a conference. Or you may recall a friend telling you that he'll "try" to contact you to set a time to help you move furniture. Chances are, it didn't happen. Why? The reason is because instead of expecting and planning for successful completion of the task, we are only concerned with "trying" – just making some attempt, no matter how minor the effort. When we fail to ride the exercise machine daily after establishing the resolution, we can absolve ourselves from feeling guilt or taking responsibility by saying, "Well, I TRIED!" This subtly destructive word saps the motivation to give our best. Replace "try" with "will," and you'll be a lot happier and more productive.

Third, think about the power of the word "CAN'T." We can do many things that we proclaim we can't. The word "can't" is often used to justify our unwillingness to take action or to blame others for our shortcomings. Usually, "can't" means "don't want to make the effort." Whenever I encounter customer service agents who claim they "can't" help me, I promptly request that they identify another person who essentially can handle the issue. In most cases, something can be done.

The next little dirty word is "SHOULD." A psychotherapist whom I know introduced me to the destructive powers of this word. Frequently, we find ourselves saying lines such as, "I should work harder," "I should go back to school," or "I should stop letting those things bother me." The word "should," like "but" and "can't," transmits signals of hesitation to our brain. It only suggests what ought to be done rather than directly generating the target behavior. In the process, because the word "should" carries strong moral overtones, we end up feeling quite guilty about our lack of subsequent action — two problems for the price of one! Unless we intend to wear diapers throughout our adult lives, we would be wise to stop "should"-ing all over ourselves! Don't say what you should do... talk about what you will do.

Lastly, let's address the word "IF." "If only we had the money" or "If only I knew how to...." In addition, how many times have you heard complainers tell you: "If only my childhood had been better" or "If only I had made wiser choices along the way, my life would be all right." The past is done – learn from it and keep pressing on. By living in the sorrows of the past rather than the promise of the future, these individuals forget to cherish the wondrous innovation of the human spirit, the prospect of change. And regardless of our age or stage in life, there is always the chance to produce. As I heard recently, "You don't stop playing because you grow old – you grow old because you stop playing." It is never too late – or too early – to pursue our dreams with vigor and purpose.

Hopefully, emboldened by this more positive vocabulary and spirit, you'll start talking and acting with full confidence. That healthy mindset is essential in pushing us to greatness, just like the blood that courses through our veins to sustain and generate life. What your mind can conceive and your heart can believe... you can achieve!

You are worthy of good things – and you must take positive risks and become an active participant in life to make it all happen. Nobody learns to ride a bicycle just by hearing a lecture alone – you have to get on and ride! You might fall a few times, but the exhilaration of ultimately accomplishing the goal (and the freedom to go as we please) is well worth the effort. Research by Harvard University professor Richard Light demonstrates that students who become involved in activities on campus typically drop out less and receive higher grades. By making new friends (especially with people sharing common interests), they find themselves enjoying the college experience more. And we all know that when we appreciate being somewhere, we're far more likely to produce better quality work. If you've ever exercised in the gym, you're well aware that the presence of a partner typically helps you to stay focused and accomplish more – and hopefully, makes the strenuous activity somewhat fun!

Right now, take a moment to identify something that you'd like to accomplish in your life. Write it down.

_____

_____

_____

_____

Next, identify one reason why achieving this goal is important to you.

_____

_____

_____

_____

OK, why do you feel that you have the ability and deserve to see it come true in your life?

_____

_____

_____

Hold onto these thoughts as you begin to prepare to pursue your vision of success.

Yet, to maximize our performance, we must identify any destructive psychological elements that could surface to tamper with our positive mindset. In particular, for many people, fears often creep in and weaken their efforts. Scientists tell us that we are born with only two fears – the fear of falling and the fear of loud sounds. If you've ever watched an infant for a long time, you've probably witnessed these innate responses. All other fears are learned, and thus, they can be overcome.

Most readers of this book can probably identify with the idea of fear of failure. Maybe you let go of a goal because you were convinced you wouldn't be successful. Possibly it was the idea that, if you put in the energy but came up short, you thought that you'd feel a lot worse than if you hadn't even bothered at all. As I have heard far too many people proclaim when rationalizing their thoughts of giving in to their fears and giving up on their goals, "But what if I fail anyway?"

Of course it's scary and emotionally risky to travel in new directions, but looking on the bright side, you have so much to potentially gain. By not even making an effort, you end up with nothing anyway – so you might as well go for it. In addition, the majority of individuals I've encountered who abandoned their dreams due to fears ended up feeling much worse years later when looking back over their lives and regretting their inaction. The streets are full of folks saddled with the "woulda, coulda, shoulda" complex, who have realized that they kept themselves from achieving their dreams in life. Instead of worrying about "if you'll fail," identify the possible rewards "when you succeed!" And, in case it doesn't work out the way you intended, you'll most likely gain skills and awareness that will prove beneficial in the long run.

One of my favorite motivational speakers, Les Brown, asks his audiences to identify the richest place in the world. While most individuals immediately mention finance-rich places such as Wall Street or the diamond mines of South Africa or the casinos of Las Vegas, Les replies that the correct answer is the graveyard. That's the place where so many great ideas end up because most people are too afraid to take the initiative to act on them. Perhaps you or someone you know has the potential to create the cure for AIDS or a strategy for revolutionizing the field of education. Take advantage of life's opportunities – and encourage your friends and family to do the same! Without the effort, you lose – and so does society.

Many people are somewhat unaware of the existence of fear of success as a significant de-motivator. Due to a history of negative situations and feedback, some individuals begin to believe that they are simply incapable of having the life of their dreams. Thus, when starting to move closer to accomplishing a goal, they engage in sabotage efforts. Some who are convinced that they cannot handle a successful relationship intentionally end up destroying it.

For others, since they fear the additional demands placed on those who do well, they do their best to elude the possibility of being identified as achievers. As a result, many people have "average" lives – not because of lack of intelligence, ability, or desire – but because that approach seems safe and easy. It's like being a "C" student – you don't feel the pressure and attention given to top students yet you're not receiving the negative treatment felt by failing individuals.

These fears typically emanate from our subconscious mind feeding us bad information. Our brains carry a kind of mental tape-recorder that constantly plays powerful messages to us that impact self-esteem and actions. These voices are a collection of ideas expressed to us throughout our lives by significant others and ourselves, and it's essential for us to analyze the audio tapes and discover their influence. If they are hurting us or holding us back, we need to record over those old tapes with more positive words that encourage us to achieve our best and feel our best. For those who heard painful messages from childhood or were blamed for family problems, it's not your fault; someone else's negativity does not have to become your reality. I'm sure that lots of other people – and hopefully you as well – see wonderful qualities in you, so let's spend more energy identifying and celebrating all that. Any athlete engaged in competition will tell you how the home team's cheering section inspires better performance, and if we're intending to venture out into new territory, it's going to be a lot easier to do it with the support of dedicated fans.

Building from that thought, here's a suggestion: After completing this book, create your own motivational tape. Think about a personal mission statement for you as well as the messages that you find to best motivate you. Perhaps you could also identify some people in your life to offer additional insights or positive words about you! Record something special and play it for yourself whenever you need a quick jump-start for your spirit. Indeed, when your car battery goes dead in the winter, you typically don't need to replace it – but rather, to grab some jumper cables and give it a boost. The same applies to our lives, as most of us go through periods when we could use a jolt of positive energy. Who would be best to do it for you... than you?

Maintaining this healthy outlook on life is a proactive process that requires your participation and energy. No one ever said that success would be easy, but the rewards of this hard work can be incredible. As a child, if you ever spent months saving money to buy that special item (maybe a video game or a new pair of gym shoes), you probably recall the happiness of eventually placing the money on the counter and purchasing it by and for yourself. Far better than just being handed the item, the feeling of satisfaction from putting in the effort and ultimately proving to be successful carries much more weight.

I hope that, with the more powerful mindset encouraged in this chapter, you're prepared to begin to concretely strategize for success. A positive attitude is an essential component but not sufficient alone – it also takes a good plan. All the tastiest ingredients won't instantly turn into a marvelous meal unless we have the right recipes. Let me share a quick story to illustrate this point. Imagine that you're on a plane, and the pilot makes the following announcement: "Ladies and gentlemen, I have good news and bad news to share. The bad news is, we don't know where we're going. But the good news is, we're making great time!" How would you feel? Well, I know lots of people who are busy racing around with smiles on their faces — but since they don't find time to clarify the direction they want to head in, they end up lost and waste plenty of time. In fact, they may never get anywhere meaningful. While Nike's old slogan "just do it" serves as a great reminder of the necessity of getting off our behinds and taking action, we need to make sure that we're doing "it" right. Thus, it is vital to get organized and create effective plans – and that's the topic of the next chapter.

But first, fill in the blank: When it comes to my attitude, I pledge to _____

_____

_____

_____

_____

in order to train my brain for more positive thought and to prepare for more beneficial action.

Things I learned or thought about when reading this chapter:

_____

_____

_____

_____

_____

_____

_____

_____

_____

_____

_____

_____

_____

BEHAVIOR
A FAILURE TO PLAN IS A PLAN FOR FAILURE!

L et's say that I told you that I had buried a wallet with $900,000 inside it next to a tree on the corner of 1st Avenue and Main Street in Tuscaloosa, Alabama. Now imagine that I shared the same information with three other people and said that the first person to locate the wallet could keep the money. The only stipulation is that contestants must drive to the location. What would you do?

Well, if you're like most people desiring more cash, you'd be pretty darn excited and ready to go get it. But, how would you proceed? See, just having a "dream" is a nice start but not sufficient for bringing it to fruition – you have to act on it and develop a meaningful strategy for achieving it.

First, in order to locate the wallet, you'd need to be willing to invest some of your time and finances. It's kind of like college. Many people drop out of college or avoid matriculating in the first place because "it costs money," or they "don't want to take out loans," or they believe that "four years is too long to wait." These individuals fail to realize the old business principle that "it takes money to make money," as well as the idea expressed by many of our parents that "anything in life worth having requires time and effort."

It's about making an investment in your future, and as you see in the box below, the typical college graduate earns about $900,000 more (the amount in that wallet) during the course of a lifetime than individuals who only possess a high school degree. So, I tell students that even if you end up with loans totaling $17,500 (the average amount for a college grad) now, it's definitely worth it; in fact, research clearly indicates that if you invested the same amount of money in the stock market as you do to attend college, you wouldn't make nearly the profit over the long haul. (By the way, it's never too late to return to school – to learn, to experience new things, or to advance your career.)

Here is the relationship between education level and lifetime earnings in the United States, based on salaries projected over a typical adult work life from age 25 to 64:

High school	$1.2 million
Bachelor's	$2.1 million
Master's	$2.5 million
PhD	$3.4 million
Professional	$4.4 million
Source: U.S. Census Bureau	

While there are no guarantees, obtaining a college degree certainly increases your likelihood of success. The same notion applies to an investment of time. If you're dedicated to accomplishing a goal, it's going to require persistent and consistent energy – and you must have the willingness to be fully engaged if you expect to achieve maximum results. By putting in the work, you're putting yourself in a better position to have your dreams come true. It took almost two years of struggle and hustle for me to finally get my first academic journal article published, but it was well worth the effort as all sorts of good things came from it.

Another critical element to consider is that we have to be ready and prepared for opportunities available to us. If the wallet deal were actually presented to you, would you have immediate access to the necessary resources to hit the road? As early civil rights pioneer Whitney Young stated, "It's better to be prepared and not get an opportunity than to get an opportunity and not be prepared." I recall a time when I could have received an excellent offer to speak for a major organization, but by not having a promotional video, I was unable to land the deal. I know so many people who do not maintain at least a small reserve of cash on hand, so when the window of opportunity opens, they lack the requisite funds to spontaneously move forward on a goal. By failing to save money today or even mentally plan out your agenda, you could be seriously inhibiting your chances for success down the line.

The case of the bamboo tree can serve as an appropriate metaphor for the benefits of making long-term investments. After the bamboo seed is planted, no visible activity takes place above ground for five years – even though the seed still must be watered and fertilized regularly during this time period to have a chance for growth later on. Then, it suddenly takes hold, miraculously breaking through the ground to grow ninety feet in about six weeks! In our lives, we often must continue to put in serious work even if we are unable to initially see the concrete gains being made. At some point, the rewards will pay off, once the roots and the foundation have been established.

But even after securing funds for gas and other expenses for the Tuscaloosa trip, you still wouldn't have everything you'd need. Instead of just getting into the car and hitting the road aimlessly, you'd be wise to obtain directions. Making maps is helpful in getting us to our geographical destinations (I ought to know, as I am directionally challenged) – and the same principle applies to our personal goals as well. If you take the time to plan out and determine the best route for getting yourself there, you're certainly in a better position to make it.

In his famous book *The Seven Habits of Highly Effective People*, Stephen Covey advises readers to "begin with the end in mind." Take a moment now to consider where you're headed. (If it's nowhere special right now, let me be your travel agent and encourage you to start making a more exciting life itinerary!) What do you envision for yourself in ten years... next year... this week? It's helpful to develop both long-range and short-range goals for yourself.

For example, as I wrote this section, I resolved to complete the book and have it published within four months. Certain steps needed to be taken to attain this goal, and I made a checklist to ensure that I fulfilled every objective and stayed on course. Just as passing certain cities on a long road trip makes us feel good about getting to our final point, knowing that we're making tangible progress on our dreams maintains the motivation as well. Having a clear timeline (i.e. finish Chapter 3 by the end of the month) and holding ourselves to it also increases the likelihood of success. Even in the midst of accomplishing the short-term goal of finishing the book, I haven't lost sight of long-term objectives, and indeed, this book serves as a springboard towards reaching other elements of that ten-year plan.

Setting and pursuing goals requires self-awareness. The better you understand yourself, your motivations, and your skills, the more likely you will be to stay focused and be successful. For example, one of my former students told our class that she needed to complete college so that all of the negative people in her life (abusive ex-boyfriends, miserable parents, discouraging teachers, etc.) who claimed she'd never amount to anything would be proven wrong. Maybe that's not the ideal reason to enroll in school, but it is clear that she can constantly draw on those feelings to sustain her drive to achieve when times get rough. Other students live in "bad" neighborhoods and want to serve as role models for their younger siblings, showing them precisely how to beat the odds. One of my colleagues resolved to purchase a beautiful new home for his mother to thank her for all the years of hard work and sacrifice for her family.

Regardless of the specific reasons, having a personal purpose is valuable in keeping us going. A friend of mine, motivational speaker Byron Garrett, uses the metaphor of the postage stamp to describe the importance of staying committed to the cause.

For mail to be delivered, the stamp must be stuck to the envelope – and we need to also stick to and with our dreams. In addition, the mail carrier promises to work in rain, sleet, snow, or hail – and again, we would benefit from a similar focus on enduring the challenging elements in order to be delivered to our ultimate destinations in life.

It is precisely these challenging elements that often mentally push many people off the path (even while they still expect their mail to arrive in the worst of weather conditions!). But when we are focused on our goals and convinced that we'll achieve them, we become more likely to intelligently design plans to use them to our advantage rather than being intimidated by these barriers. Years ago, Gary Barnett, then the head coach of the Northwestern University football team, faced a situation that required the use of his famed motivational tactics. Remembering that Northwestern's next opponent, the Iowa Hawkeyes, painted the visitors' locker room pink to distract the other team, Barnett conjured up a brilliant plan. To prepare the players and even make them feel as if that locker room in Iowa were their home, he covered the walls of their own locker room on campus with the same pink color the week before — and his squad ended up surprisingly winning in a landslide. Our own life dilemmas can be creatively conquered as well.

Yes, we will face roadblocks and setbacks every step along the way in life. That statement is not intended to discourage you from making the investment, but rather, to help you understand the challenge and to anticipate these hurdles so that you can better plan to overcome them. It's an intriguing fact that some track athletes who specialize in the hurdles event can actually run that race faster than they can cover the same distance without the hurdles. The presence of the hurdles actually propels them to push harder. If you become aware of the possible obstacles in your way, they won't surprise or deter you – only embolden you to keep going. As someone once told me, "obstacles are only footstools to achieve greater things."

I recall when my car had a flat tire while I was driving alone in South Africa a few years ago. With no one around to help me, I started to panic. I had never up to that point changed a tire and just assumed that I wouldn't ever need that skill, as long as AAA was a quick phone call away. But clearly, I was wrong. And I had to get busy and figure out what to do. And so I did. Now, the task might have taken me a bit of time, but realizing that I had no option but success, I maintained focus and developed a new skill that has subsequently saved me time and money. I beamed with pride about being able to handle the situation and still utilize that memory as a reminder of the power of positive thinking and the need to see challenges as opportunities for gain.

When I was hired for the first time to work with a professional sports team, I knew that many of these superstars would be somewhat skeptical about taking advice from a non-athlete whom they knew little about. I felt as if my initial group motivational sessions were quite productive, but I still could sense that the players held back some degree of respect. Recognizing the popularity of hip-hop culture in the locker room, I sat down one afternoon and composed a spoken word poem that incorporated the players' names and roles. I clearly knew the risks involved, since a poor performance would have been so embarrassing and could have truly damaged my reputation. But, it needed to be done – and delivered with complete confidence and conviction. In the end, the poem drew tremendously positive response, and as one player mentioned to me a few days later, "When you took that chance and did your piece, that was when I came to really respect you."

So, we need planning, positivity, perseverance, and preparedness. But perhaps it all boils down to one fundamental additional "p" word: purpose. What's your purpose? According to Helen Keller, "Many people have a wrong idea of what constitutes true happiness. It is not attained through self-gratification, but through fidelity to a worthy purpose." What is it that you believe that you are here on Earth to accomplish? What do you want said about you at your funeral? That last idea might sound a bit morbid, but in reality, we all have a finite amount of time to live. Two close friends of mine teach college courses on death, and they both contend that by exploring this difficult subject, students actually begin to live life with greater purpose and passion.

I have determined that my primary purpose is to make the world a better place in any way possible. You see, years before I was born, both of my parents had cancer. In fact, after undergoing radiation treatment, my father was informed that he would be unable to conceive any more children. Well, I guess that my presence shows how doctors can be wrong! I inform people that I am not an "accident" – cars have accidents – I am a "surprise" child. Furthermore, my parents were told that they ought to have an abortion, as it was predicted that the fetus would not develop properly and that something could definitely turn out wrong. Basically, I shouldn't be here... but I am. Therefore, I know that my existence must have some sense of purpose – and that if I could be granted the miracle of life, it was my obligation to pursue whatever avenues I could in order to improve the quality of life for others.

Even if you currently have a successful professional career, you still may feel that you have another aspiration out there that needs to be accomplished. Now, some people tell me that they don't yet know their purpose. That's not necessarily a problem. In fact, I know too many individuals who rush into a career path without carefully considering if it's really their passion. The key is to do something now that grants you the chance to ultimately find that purpose. If you're unsure, think about a few things that you truly enjoy or might consider as your life goals. For example, perhaps you like working with children or have pondered the notion of starting your own theatre company. Don't worry – you don't have to commit to that idea for the rest of your life, just to consider it. With those thoughts in mind, go out and get information related to those possibilities. Talk to someone who operates a playhouse. Volunteer at the local school. Read books on the subject. Complete an internship. Do something!

You see, just by obtaining information and experiences, you'll eventually know if it's right for you. And even if you discover that you're not really interested in it, you've most likely gained meaningful additions to your personal tool belt of talents in the process. For my entire childhood, I wanted to be a TV sports broadcaster. I'd actually practice by announcing when mom brought food to the table! Although I decided to change my career goals to education, the skills that I gained as an announcer in high school and college have clearly been helpful in my teaching and speaking endeavors.

At age 20, when I discovered that the Sociology Department offered a combined undergraduate and graduate degree program, I decided to apply for it. No one else had attempted it in fifteen years, but I figured that I was up for the challenge. At the time, I only thought that I wanted to be a youth worker. But in the end, armed with these credentials, I was able to start teaching college classes part time – and what had been a wonderful side addition to my life has ended up becoming the centerpiece of my professional career!

By pursuing life with passion, we learn all sorts of new things about ourselves that can change our futures. Being active also allows others to see our skills and even notice gifts within us that we hadn't even perceived. Incredible new opportunities and mentoring situations can be the result. With respect to being a motivational speaker, it was by putting myself out there to work with kids that allowed for someone else to see a future for me that I had not previously recognized. I never even knew that people could make serious money doing presentations. But when I was offered a chance to conduct a workshop at a national conference, I jumped at the chance and soon realized that I possessed a certain talent in this area.

Contrary to the popular myth, opportunity rarely just comes knocking on our door. For the most part, we need to go out and track down opportunities, taking advantage of situations that could provide us with the chance to learn, to grow, to network, and to discover our many talents. As far as I know, we only get one chance at life - and we can't get out of it alive. So, we might as well grant ourselves the permission to pursue our dreams. Again, even if the path is diverted or we realize that we aren't best suited for a particular career or interest, just the idea of the passionate pursuit allows us to realize our fullest potential. Besides, it's far more fun this way.

I need to include a note of warning here. One of the most emotionally painful realizations that people can make is that as they begin to transform their lives for the better, others often begin to resent them or even attempt to sabotage their progress. In many cases, it's family and friends who can be the worst offenders. Those individuals might be jealous, because our advances remind them of their own failures. They may not be intentionally and consciously trying to hurt you, but rather, could be feeling the burden of their own painful lives. Don't let them get you down — you have the power to define yourself and your existence, to write your own life story. When discussing this issue with my students, some report that when they started making progress in life, they felt compelled to totally break free from those people who wished them harm; others elected to maintain the relationships at a distance. It's up to you to do what seems best - but just be aware that some changes will probably have to take place along the way.

Indeed, every step forward involves some degree of loss. When you move to a new city, you have to leave friends and places behind. The lifestyle of the rich and famous almost always yields a significant loss of personal time and privacy. The goal, of course, is to maximize our gains and draw strength and insight from the losses. It is important to be aware of the potential sacrifices that may need to be made to accomplish our goals, so that we're not thrown off course when encountering them.

On a positive note, every one of us has a dedicated group of supporters who deeply wish for our success – and by identifying and consulting with those individuals, we can take advantage of these incredible resources. I've been hearing a number of people talk recently about the notion of a personal "Board of Directors." Just like a company that uses distinguished individuals to guide its direction, it is helpful for all of us to seek out people in our lives who can be mentors and members of our support systems. We're not experts in everything, and by bouncing ideas off of others, we subsequently gain the benefit of their wisdom and experience. I'd even recommend including someone on the Board with little direct knowledge of your fields of interest, as a true "outsider" can bring a unique point of view and spot important things others might have ignored or taken for granted.

One young man e-mailed me recently after a presentation and proclaimed, "You may not know it, but you're part of my personal Board now. Since you told us to stay in touch with you, I intend to ask for your advice on a regular basis." If you plan to start a business, who can be a good source of information for you regarding financial issues? Advertising? Personnel matters? You may know a great deal, but others who have been there and done that can add something valuable; besides, most people love talking about themselves and their talents! And since we have two eyes and two ears but only one mouth, we'd be wise to watch and listen twice as much as we talk. As all athletes will tell you, matching up against someone with supposedly superior skills typically pushes them to raise the level of their own game. While it may be humbling to interact with others who have accomplished "more," we'd be wise to take advantage of the opportunity.

I want to share a particular story in order to summarize key concepts addressed thus far in this chapter. One day, an old man went to the neighborhood park and began digging in the middle of the field. Soon, a crowd of young people gathered around to observe. One of the teenage girls, known for her abrasive and arrogant manner, shouted out to the elder: "Silly old man, don't you realize that you are planting the Acacia tree? That tree takes seventy-five years to grow. How stupid you are, for you will never see it grow!" The man paused for a brief moment and then firmly raised himself upright, as best as his creaking bones would permit. He looked down at the girl and firmly responded, "You may be right, but if I don't plant this tree, YOU will never see it grow." Others may doubt our intentions – and our goals may take a long time to come to fruition – but, for so many reasons, the work must be done.

As Tommy Lasorda, the former manager of the Los Angeles Dodgers, once proclaimed, "In baseball and in business, there are three types of people: those who make it happen; those who watch it happen; and those who wonder what happened." Yes, to make it happen, it will take time, hard work, and sacrifice – and sometimes, we must start at the bottom and utilize both inspiration and perspiration in order to rise to the top. In the words of Marian Wright Edelman, the brilliant president of the Children's Defense Fund, "There's no free lunch. Don't feel entitled to anything you don't sweat and struggle for." Success in life does require real effort, as you don't get out of life merely what you want, but rather, what you earn.

To illustrate this point, I want to discuss how, contrary to popular belief, doing well in life is not primarily determined by how "intelligent" you are. In many cases, it's more a function of how well you devise a meaningful game plan that leads to greater chances of success. Herbert Walberg has conducted numerous studies of super-achieving students and concludes that the top grades usually go to the students who "work smarter," not always to the individuals with the highest IQs. For years, despite investing considerable time and effort, I struggled to improve my golf skills. After finally deciding to take lessons from an expert, I learned all sorts of new and helpful techniques. I'm still obligated to train more to continue improving my performance, but with a solid foundation from which to start, this work will now end up being far more fruitful. By "working smarter," I elevated my game and found increased enjoyment from playing!

I have encountered so many students who reported a sincere desire to raise their grades, yet they often ended up repeating the same patterns because they lacked the knowledge of how to study better. In some cases, these individuals worked considerably harder, but their failure to work smarter was the problem. Doing more of a wrong thing does not yield better results. A quick suggestion of working smarter when studying for tests would be to pair up with a classmate and have each person make up a practice exam on the material. Then, swap exams and pretend it's the real deal. After completing the tests, you can go over the answers together and help each other to learn the information. In addition to teaching one another (which is the best way to learn, according to educational psychologists), the process of devising the practice tests helps us to clarify important material and prepare for the actual experience. Regardless of our personal situation, we can all benefit from working smarter.

We must also keep in mind the scientific research indicating that significant behavioral or attitudinal transformation usually takes about 21 days of consistent performance to become habit. Thus, while we often become initially excited about making changes, we forget that this new behavior must be practiced over and over again before it can be fully internalized. Just doing something for a few days is not sufficient enough – you have to keep at it.

A few years back, I resolved to lose weight and get myself back into better shape. I didn't feel that I was operating at my physical best, and as a result, I had not been achieving my ultimate level of productivity. A car with watered-down gas or sandbags in the trunk is not going to run as fast as it ought to. A significant part of this healthier living campaign involved a daily run on the treadmill. Now, to be honest, I started off pretty slow – and that's OK. Too many people fail to take that first step in pursuing their dreams out of concerns for how far they will need to travel or how awkward they might look initially. Keep in mind that everybody appears clumsy on the first attempt to ride a bicycle, and no child reaching the gates of Disneyland ever turned back around and went home because the trip to get there had been lengthy. If it's important to us, we put in the work and celebrate the investment. We all know that soup tests better the longer it simmers, so appreciate the process.

At the beginning, I established the target of a half-mile run, followed by twenty minutes of slower walking. Maybe that's not much, but I had to start with something realistic so that I would not become discouraged and abandon the journey. Some people want to make their goals happen so quickly that they give up too soon when unable to attain the ultimate prize overnight. Then, I raised the bar a little bit each time to challenge myself to go further. Every day was a real struggle, and while I recognized that hard work and sacrifice would be involved, I had been hoping for a slightly easier start. I felt that I was giving everything I had physically just to hit the daily goal.

After a week of exercise, I decided to stretch myself to run a full mile. Even though I was somewhat excited about the idea of reaching this symbolic plateau, I remained slightly worried that I would fall short. The day before had been a real pain, as I barely completed the final two-tenths of a mile. However, as I neared the mile marker, I literally felt my body break through the proverbial wall and come out refreshed on the other side. It was as if all the physical and emotional burdens that had been weighing me down had been miraculously lifted. I ran for another twenty minutes without any trouble, and actually, started to enjoy it all for the first time.

I found some meaningful parallels between this experience and our daily lives. I was reminded once again that we can accomplish so much more than we think is possible for us – and that time and stick-to-it-tiveness are necessary ingredients to make it happen. No one could have convinced me that I'd run two miles within a week of resuming exercise, but by pushing beyond my perceived limits, I discovered so much about myself and felt tremendous pride. And perhaps more importantly, I learned something about the self-imposed walls we often create that keep us from realizing our fullest potential. We have to be vigilant in rooting out any internal or external forces that might be inhibiting our growth.

One aspect of life that negatively affects many people is money management, and it is critical for readers to consider ways to enhance their financial literacy. It's sad that people joke about their lack of financial skills ("I'm just not good with money" or "I don't know much about those issues"), as if they would ever joke about their lack of literacy in other areas ("I just don't read well"). Having financial resources allows us to maintain the power to make better decisions in our lives. Consider the example of a recent college graduate who ends up spending a fortune on a new car to celebrate his accomplishments. First of all, the car depreciates about 30-40% just by driving it off the lot (why not spend a good portion of those funds investing in something that will earn money rather than automatically losing it?). But now saddled with another debt (in addition to student loans, credit cards, etc.), he's less likely to be able to leave a job that makes him sick someday because he cannot afford to do so. On a similar note, a friend of mine once told me to make sure that, in addition to a main job, I ought to always have side income that could be used to cover my rent or mortgage. That way, one is never beholden to a job and could still take care of the most central expense in case something drastic ever happened.

Do you know the difference between a pair of sneakers that cost

$30 and ones selling for $130? In most cases, the difference is simply $100. These higher-end shoes are marked way up due to advertising and fees paid to superstar athletes who endorse them, even though they are essentially the same product as the less expensive version. I'm always saddened when watching young parents spend oodles of dollars on pricey sneakers for their newborn children, as if the baby really needed these items that could be replaced by much-needed educational materials!

That's not to say that we ought not allow ourselves to enjoy the finer things in life – only that we would be wise to carefully check to be certain that it's really worth the extra money. For years, I purchased decent used cars that looked good enough and ran well. The cars weren't the flashiest, but they served the purpose. Ultimately, when my peers were struggling at the end of the month and could not splurge on nice dinners or mini-vacations whenever they wanted, I was able to be spontaneous. Then, after saving enough money, I bought my first dream car (it was still used) with cash – why bother losing thousands of dollars in interest?

By the way, someone who just makes the minimum payment on a typical credit card will find that the $2000 purchase takes about ten years to pay off, with a total interest amount of over $1200. If you just add $25 more per month to the payment, the balance disappears in just two years and ends up being over $800 less in interest. Saving money is a state of mind.

An old adage contends that "a closed mouth doesn't get fed." The underlying principle of this statement can be easily applied to financial matters. Having accidentally left my battery charger in the hotel on a recent speaking trip, I went to the cell phone store to purchase a new one. When I approached the counter, I simply asked if the company had a "discount for good customers." It was said playfully, but considering that I had been using their service for years, I had serious intentions. The service agent knocked $10 off the price. It doesn't hurt to ask.

On that same trip, I started a friendly conversation with the woman sitting next to me on the flight and asked her profession. She was an administrator at a college and had just assumed the new responsibility of planning and implementing a course to orient new students to higher education. I simply inquired if she had selected any textbooks, and when told that nothing had been chosen yet, I handed her a copy of the book you are reading now. In the end, she purchased a bunch of copies for her staff.

As another example, in one study, 57% of men but only 7% of women negotiated for higher salaries upon receiving their first job offer. Instead of just accepting what was given to them, these individuals ended up adding about $4000 to their salaries! Others make wise financial moves by asking for relocation expenses. The worst that the boss can say is no, so why not believe in yourself enough to get what you are worth?

My good friend Michael Walton, an international track star and motivational speaker for youth, uses the analogy of the bank account to illustrate the points raised in this chapter. If you've been regularly depositing money into your account, you can expect funds to be there when you decide to splurge on the new outfit for the summer; the opposite is obviously true in the reverse situation, where you can't expect to buy anything if the balance is zero (and the credit is poor). The same principle applies to life. If, for example, you desire to be a famous singer, you'll need to make deposits into your career account – by practicing consistently, developing contacts with people in the industry, creating promotional materials, etc. You've got to be ready at any time to produce, and continuously striving to enhance your craft and your experience allows you to be at your best. As Michael says, he won't be able to win the gold medal simply out of desire alone. Thus, he puts in the hard work training every day to ensure that when he steps to the line at his next race, he has all the resources necessary to cross the finish line in first place.

Let's play with this metaphor a little bit. What kind of deposits and withdrawals do you make in life, and how do you feel about all that?

_____

_____

_____

_____

_____

Ultimately, our best efforts result from positivity, planning, preparation, persistence, passion, and purpose. Now that we have recognized the benefits of maintaining a positive attitude and initiating successful strategies, we must consider ways to preserve the spirit and live it enthusiastically every day. That's the theme of the next chapter.

Fill in this blank: When it comes to making my behavior work better on my behalf, I pledge to:

_____

_____

_____

_____

_____

_____

_____

_____

_____

_____

_____

_____

_____

Things I learned or thought about when reading this chapter:

_____

_____

_____

_____

_____

_____

_____

_____

_____

_____

_____

_____

OWNERSHIP
HOW TO STAY ON FIRE... WITHOUT BURNING OUT!

A few years ago, a man named Billie Bob Harrell, Jr. held onto a fantasy that many of us probably could relate to. While laboring for years in a somewhat less-than-fulfilling job as a shelf stocker, Billie Bob dreamed of hitting it big with the lottery so he could better support his wife and three children. And when turning in the winning ticket for a $31 million grand prize, he was catapulted into fame and fortune.

I imagine that practically every reader of this book has uttered the phrase, "If only I could just win the lottery," anticipating automatic and permanent joy coming from these riches. Yet, because he was unprepared for the emotional and practical consequences of wealth, everything spiraled downhill for Billie Bob. The lavish lifestyle he started quickly ended up siphoning off all his winnings. Within the year, he was divorced – and in the following year, he put a gun to his chest and fired a fatal bullet. This true story is not an isolated example, as tales of unhappy Lotto winners abound; it's not by accident that suicide rates among the rich surpass the numbers for less wealthy segments of the population. Too often, money and pressure take control of their lives, and attaining a financial dream does not necessarily equate with perpetual happiness. When we no longer strive to continue growing and achieving, we begin the process of a slow death.

Perhaps happiness in life is achieved through the combination of being able to look in our rearview mirror and identify goals we have already accomplished while preserving enthusiasm for new challenges and growth opportunities unfolding ahead of us. Maintaining a healthy lifestyle is the key. To offer an analogy, a beautiful new car doesn't run nearly as well or last as long when the owner does not engage in regular maintenance efforts. We have to stay on fire... without burning out!

Thus, the purpose of this book is not to persuade you to seek some temporary alterations to your life, but more significantly, to challenge you to adopt successful overall plans for *how you live*. To truly fulfill our purpose requires a general system of regular success, not just flashes of greatness. Some people, after being inspired by a motivational speaker or book, immediately decide to pursue a particular dream. Yet, if they fail to meaningfully prepare for all the changes that will occur when pursuing a new goal, the prospects of success are diminished. The point is to develop life agendas that will sustain you for the long haul.

Let's take an example. Think of some significant change that you would like to see in your own life. OK, now consider all the steps you must take in order to accomplish this task. While I'm sure that you've just outlined a realistic framework, you might have neglected other dimensions of your life outside of this goal alone that may have to be adjusted as well. For instance, with the time demands involved in pursuing this plan, how will your family life or friendships be affected? Will you have to endure any other sacrifices? True ownership means taking charge of your entire way of being and planning out ways to maintain balance and optimal life productivity. Thus, this chapter builds on the concepts addressed in the previous one by encouraging readers to go beyond making plans for a singular goal, instead striving to gain total autonomy over their lives as a whole.

Taking control of our destiny means accepting full responsibility for our behavior and mental state as well as for the consequences of our actions. It is disappointing to me when people say things such as, "He made me mad" or "I just couldn't help myself," as these statements indicate a willingness to give up power over our emotions and our behavior to outside forces. Once, a young woman in my youth program in Chicago commented to me, "It just happened - I got pregnant." Well, dear readers, although I don't teach courses in human sexuality, I still feel qualified enough to assert that the pregnancy didn't just "happen" to her out of nowhere!

Assuming full ownership for our lives also means taking advantage of life's blessings each day. Today is the first day of the rest of your life, and you have the power to lose it or use it. Once the clock strikes midnight tonight, you'll never get today back - so hopefully, you'll be able to say that you used it to the fullest!

This ownership also demands that we pursue and expect excellence from ourselves in all aspects of our lives. I firmly believe that allowing ourselves to slack in any critical domain establishes the mental framework of tolerating less than our best – and this spirit can carry over into other areas. Be your best at all times!

Every day, we face situations that test our resolve or provide a chance for real growth – yet, we often either ignore or intentionally resist them. Right now, create a list of a few significant things that you did yesterday.

OK, now consider additional actions you could have taken that might have provided extra life value for you. It's not only what we do that matters, but also what we don't do – and clearly, not to decide or act represents a powerful decision that preserves the status quo.

As a student, did you take full advantage of the opportunities available to you to learn and develop? For example, did you attend the free public lecture on campus, even though it wasn't required? If not, you might have missed out on an incredible experience that could have inspired you or offered a valuable contact person for your career. What would it have cost you versus what could have gained by attending – and what did you do instead, spend a few more meaningless minutes on the website myspace.com?

As an employee, did you maximize your time at the job, remembering that people are constantly watching us? It's not always about our performance on the big presentation or the major report that determines our promotion possibilities. Sometimes, it's the way we handle the mundane tasks or proactively pursue new activities that can make the difference.

As a romantic partner or parent, did you pay close attention to all the verbal and non-verbal responses provided by loved ones yesterday that indicated a particular need or desire? Did you go above and beyond to do something special, for no other reason than to produce a smile on that person's face?

You see, we often wait for major events to summon the courage to make significant change. But by failing to pursue the possibilities within each day, we limit the opportunities that could be available to us tomorrow. You don't start training for the Olympics a week before the competition. When you don't seize the day - every day - you're squandering precious chances to meet new people, gain vital skills, and develop confidence that can ultimately increase chances for success down the road.

So, let's practice how to take advantage of life. Right now, look around and identify one opportunity that is being presented to you (besides this wonderful book!) that could enhance your life and open doors to a brighter today and tomorrow. Maybe it's a hobby that you once thought about pursuing but kept pushing to the side. Or perhaps it's making that phone call to the local college to register for a financial empowerment class. Now, think about what you have to gain by going for it at this time - and what you continue to lose (now and in the future) by remaining passive. Opportunities are all around you, so start with this one and strategize for making it happen!

It's all about mindset. One of the most significant qualities of successful individuals and teams is the competitive spirit that compels them to see winning as the only option. Conversely, those who play "not to lose" down the stretch of a game usually end up falling short of their goals because they are not controlling their own destiny or performing with complete confidence. I recall watching Tiger Woods on TV during his final U.S. Amateur championship many years ago. Down by a wide margin with only five holes to play, Tiger's chances of winning were considered slim by even the commentators who had initially predicted an easy win for him. But, his name was not chosen just for image – but rather, to reflect his fiery, indomitable spirit. Seeing the determination in his eyes, I knew that Tiger would play to win. And he did win. Failure was not even a possibility.

To stay on fire without burning out requires both passion and purpose. When we're actively engaged in something that matters to us, the labor doesn't seem so bad. Indeed, I spend considerable hours "on the job" and continue to put in extra time to improve my craft because I love what I do. Something in our lives – whether it's the pursuit of a career goal, the raising of a child, the dedication to a hobby, or whatever – needs to be so important and enjoyable to us that full engagement brings us excitement and pleasure.

Before being elected as the President of South Africa, Nelson Mandela was a true activist whose fervent work against apartheid led the government to imprison him for 27 years. During that time, he could have gained his release – if only he would have agreed to abandon his cause of seeking to dismantle the oppressive state. Of course, he refused to become silent, and instead, remained committed to his principles. In the end, his heroic stance proved to transform a nation and inspire the world.

Next, I firmly believe that knowing ourselves helps us to better appreciate how we function and what changes could be made to improve our lives. Ownership of our lives also means that we're honest about real weaknesses. Rather than avoiding these areas of discomfort, self-directed individuals view weaknesses as challenges to be overcome. I know that I do not possess the greatest organizational skills, and my office often remains messy. While I basically manage to find everything, I recently recognized that I could be more productive. So I resolved to work on it and now ask my students to help me in the growth process! Ultimately, perceived weaknesses can actually become strengths for us. For example, I tend to have a high-energy personality, and if I like something, I really like it. A long time ago, I decided that I might not be able to control the use of alcohol or other drugs if I started to indulge – and therefore, I have never permitted myself to become drunk or high. I prefer to be in charge of myself, and the outcome is a healthier lifestyle overall.

Simply put, for real and sustained ownership to occur, individuals must be proactive about addressing potential concerns rather than being reactive to problems when they surface. If you've ever played basketball, you know that it takes more physical and mental energy to be the defender than the offensive player who directs the process, even when the two athletes are traveling the exact same steps. Also, if you've ever driven behind someone who is showing the way, you probably felt much more uncomfortable than the lead driver because you don't have full control over the lane changes, directions, and speed. Take charge and be the driver of your own car of life!

Thus, I have included the following "personality test" on the next page and hope that you will find it to be a meaningful way of understanding more about yourself.

Read each item and assign points based on the "correctness" of the three responses for your life, using up to ten points per question. The more it applies to you, the more points you give – with the sum of all three scores being no more than ten. For example, as demonstrated in the following sample questions, the respondent believed that the first answer was very true (6 points), the second one somewhat true (3 points), and the third one not very true (1 point). The three scores across must add up to ten.

But before you begin, jot down some reflections about your own personality:

_____

_____

_____

_____

_____

_____

PERSONALITY TEST
Sample Questions 1-5

1. I would describe myself as a person who is...

`6` friendly, open and sees some good in almost everyone.

`3` full of energy, sure of myself and one who sees chances others miss.

`1` careful and fair and one who stands by what he or she believes to be right.

2. Most of the time I find myself being...

`4` the "nice" one who is almost always willing to help others.

`6` the "strong" one who points out the way for others.

`0` the "thinking" one who studies things carefully before acting.

3. Most of the time I am...

`3` a person who cares and is quick to help other people.

`4` a person who is quick to see chances to get something for myself.

`3` a practical person who is careful not to rush into things before I am ready.

4. People who know me best see me as a person who can be counted on...

`5` to trust them and be loyal to them.

`4` to want to get ahead and willing to take charge.

`1` to do what I think is right and not be pushed around by what others think.

5. When I am at my best, I most enjoy...

`3` seeing others benefit from what I have been able to do for them.

`4` having others turn to me to lead and guide them.

`3` being my own boss and doing things for myself and by myself.

A   `21` *(add 1-5)*   `21` *(add 1-5)*   `8` *(add 1-5)*

PERSONALITY TEST
Questions 1-5

1. I would describe myself as a person who is...

☐ friendly, open and sees some good in almost everyone.

☐ full of energy, sure of myself and one who sees chances others miss.

☐ careful and fair and one who stands by what he or she believes to be right.

2. Most of the time I find myself being...

☐ the "nice" one who is almost always willing to help others.

☐ the "strong" one who points out the way for others.

☐ the "thinking" one who studies things carefully before acting.

3. Most of the time I am...

☐ a person who cares and is quick to help other people.

☐ a person who is quick to see chances to get something for myself.

☐ a practical person who is careful not to rush into things before I am ready.

4. People who know me best see me as a person who can be counted on...

☐ to trust them and be loyal to them.

☐ to want to get ahead and willing to take charge.

☐ to do what I think is right and not be pushed around by what others think.

5. When I am at my best, I most enjoy...

☐ seeing others benefit from what I have been able to do for them.

☐ having others turn to me to lead and guide them.

☐ being my own boss and doing things for myself and by myself.

A ☐ *(add 1-5)*   ☐ *(add 1-5)*   ☐ *(add 1-5)*

PERSONALITY TEST
Questions 6-10

6. When I run into trouble in what I am doing, I am most likely to...

☐ give up what I am doing in order to keep peace.

☐ argue for my right to do it anyway

☐ become very careful and make sure of what is going on.

7. When someone strongly disagrees with me, I usually...

☐ give in and do it their way.

☐ challenge them right away and argue as hard as I can.

☐ stay cool and back off until I'm sure of where I stand.

8. If I'm not getting what I want from others, I usually...

☐ keep hoping and trusting that things will work themselves out in time.

☐ push harder to get what I want.

☐ stop dealing with the person and look somewhere else for what I want.

9. When things aren't going well in my life, I usually...

☐ talk to others and get their advice.

☐ waste no time feeling sorry for myself and see it as a challenge for myself to overcome.

☐ take time to carefully analyze the situation and make a plan for change.

10. When someone has done something so that I can't trust them anymore, I usually...

☐ feel sad that the relationship did not work.

☐ get angry and take steps to even the score.

☐ figure out what went wrong and how to not let it happen again.

B ☐ *(add 6-10)*   ☐ *(add 6-10)*   ☐ *(add 6-10)*

After you finish question five, add the scores in each column going down and place the numbers in the square boxes for the row labeled A. You will end up with three different scores, which should total 50 when adding across. Do the same thing for questions 6–10. When you have finished with this task, continue reading for the meaning of the results.

Each column represents a different personality type. People with very high scores in the first column are what I label the "Kind Kangaroos." These individuals typically have caring hearts and spend considerable energy helping others. On the positive side, they tend to have close friendships and to be supportive people who are very well liked by others. However, Kind Kangaroos must be careful about being taken advantage of or focusing so much on everyone else's needs that they neglect their own. Kind Kangaroos usually avoid conflict and might give in rather than fight for their beliefs.

The middle column is represented by the "Leaderly Lions." As evidenced by the name, individuals with high scores here tend to be take-charge folks who are unafraid of challenge. These leadership skills often serve them well in accomplishing goals, but there is a potential tendency to be bossy or believe that their way is the best way. They usually enjoy conflict and, in contrast with Kangaroos, care little if others don't like them.

Lastly, we have the "Analytical Aardvarks," people who prefer to "look before they leap." By carefully checking out situations before making decisions, they rarely regret the eventual choices they make. However, sometimes this waiting period leads them to miss out on valuable life opportunities.

Many people find themselves with very high numbers in one of the categories, showing a strong identification with that personality type. Other profiles reflect a combination of characteristics that may shift based on the particular context. Some respondents tend to be evenly distributed between the three characters, and these individuals tend to be "go with the flow" types who can easily adjust to changing situations.

So, do the results of this little test accurately reflect your personality? Ah, but there is a surprise! The numbers for Row A (the larger numbers after questions 1–5) correspond to who you are when things are going well for you. Row B (the scores for questions 6–10) is all about how you behave when life isn't treating you so kindly. Are the numbers similar (indicating a fairly balanced and consistent personality), or are you a totally different person when you're not getting what you want? For many people, the numbers in the middle column vary greatly, with higher scores in Row B indicating the possibility of a temper or lower scores revealing an aversion to conflict. It's also common to see much higher numbers in the third column in Row B, suggesting that these individuals prefer to be left alone when upset.

There are no right or wrong answers. The point is for you to hopefully gain some insight into the kind of person you might be. By being more cognizant of this reality, you possess greater awareness of the possible risks associated with that personality type and, if you so choose, you can make desired adjustments. When processing this exercise during my workshops, lots of individuals have appreciated the chance to obtain this feedback, as it often helped to explain some behavioral patterns they experienced but didn't quite understand. Conversely, you might find yourself happy with the results as they are.

It would be helpful for people in romantic relationships or for teams to take this personality test and share the results. Perhaps you'll discover that the reason for tension between you and a co-worker is due to the fact that you like to talk out problems while initially he prefers to cool down and think it through before engaging in dialogue. Without this knowledge, the situation could become exacerbated, with both parties frustrated at the other individual.

It also might be intriguing to ask someone else to score you in order to learn how others perceive your personality. It's quite possible that we want to see ourselves in a particular light, but we just may be engaging in self-deceit. A concept called Johari's Window speaks to the notion that some aspects of our personality remain invisible to ourselves while being quite evident to others (just as some parts are known to us but remain hidden from others). Therefore, it's beneficial to seek out others' perspectives to learn about our potential strengths and weaknesses. As mentioned earlier in this chapter, it can be emotionally difficult to discover these shortcomings or be reminded of possible improvements to be pursued. But, the goal is to make yourself the best resource possible... for yourself!

This way, we can keep growing. We are all works in progress, and the day you think that you "know it all" is probably the day you begin to die. No one is perfect – but we often expect others to be perfect. We wouldn't be satisfied hearing the dentist proclaim that she "tried" after extracting the wrong tooth! One report claimed that if hospitals correctly handled 99.99% of baby deliveries, 16 newborns would be going home each day with the wrong parents! Thus, we can challenge ourselves to never accept anything less than our best. (By the way, practice makes... nope, not perfect. Practice makes better, as we can always better our supposed best.) A great educator named Dr. Johnnetta Cole reminds students, "Show me someone content with mediocrity, and I'll show you someone destined for failure."

Thus, it is essential that we remain humble enough to realize that changes might need to be made in order to achieve our goals. I often hear people claim that "I can't change that part of me – it's who I am." Not true. The behavior may be who you are at that moment, but what you choose to be is a different story. For example, one student used that line of reasoning to explain why he felt incapable of doing anything with his anger other than fight. Clearly, he had grown up in a family and community that valued the ability to "kick butt" more than conflict resolution skills, but that reality does not mean that he is obligated to maintain the same pattern forever. You can change, if you believe that it is in your best interest.

Now, I know what some of you are thinking: "I don't want to change who I am. I don't want to be a fake or to allow others to influence me that way!" If you really believe that your behaviors simply reflect who you will always be, ask yourself if you're the exact same person now as you were at age 8. Hopefully, you've changed in lots of ways. It is possible to hold onto many of your core principles and traits while allowing yourself to add new components to your personality. The famous saying that "the only constant in life is change" holds true. We're constantly evolving, and it's wise to appreciate opportunities to keep moving and growing to continuously strive to be at our best. If you always do what you've always done, you'll always get what you've always got. After all, malaria can only grow in stagnant water.

I'm always amazed when individuals proudly proclaim that they "don't care at all" what people think of them. Of course, I understand that, in some ways, they are asserting how this thick skin keeps them from being bothered or hurt by others' comments. Perhaps that's a good thing. Yet, I believe that there are deeply dangerous consequences to this state of mind. First of all, what others think of us will affect our relationships and the opportunities that could be presented. If we're unaware that people don't like or respect something about us, we will be unable to address those concerns and possibly repair these connections. Typically, I find that people who say they don't care what others think of them are less likely to put in the effort to successfully work through challenges with colleagues or co-workers, instead resorting to negative behaviors. Contrary to popular belief, the majority of people who are fired from jobs or miss out on promotions are not losing because of poor job performance, but rather, because of their inability to get along with others.

Maintaining a positive image among others is professionally valuable in the long run. A sociologist named Mark Granovetter has written extensively about the notion of the "strength of weak ties," suggesting that the informal social networks that we participate in have a tremendous influence in our lives. For example, it is estimated that up to 80% of jobs are filled through word-of-mouth, not classified ads. Knowing more people – and having a good reputation – can significantly enhance our quality of life.

Finally, we ought to care about what others think of us because we just don't know it all. Years ago, during a particularly arrogant adolescent time period, I resisted taking a good look at myself and how I had been treating others. Nobody could tell me anything, and my relationships suffered tremendously. I was fortunate that a good friend was persistent in her efforts to inform me of my shortcomings, and I eventually and fortunately turned my attitude and behavior around. I would encourage readers to be open to what people have to say, even if it is difficult to hear. We don't have to agree with them, but the information could be quite meaningful.

Encouraging ourselves to live outside the box means that we can encounter new experiences that expand our horizons. I recall hearing a youth worker talk about getting his inner-city students to play squash for the first time. Upon seeing the court and the other players who looked nothing like him, one young man proclaimed, "This game is not for us." But, after some prodding from the staff, he took the risk – and ended up as the city champion in the sport a few years later! So, if you're the kind of person who hesitates to sample new cuisine, go ahead and give it a chance; you have little to lose and a whole new world of exciting tastes to gain. If you're a huge fan of alternative music, why not at least pick up a jazz CD sometime and take a listen? It's not necessarily about Thai food or Count Basie, but rather, the idea of being open to all sorts of new possibilities and new ways to look at the world and yourself. And as a result, life becomes more exciting – and you develop the state of mind that generates innovation and improvements.

To keep a fire going, one needs to progressively add more wood and make adjustments without smothering the flame. We don't have to radically change everything about ourselves at one time – just as it's usually preferable to continue looking for the best spots to place the wood and staying close to the fire pit to monitor and regulate.

Finally, staying on fire without burning out requires daily devotion to functioning in an optimal and holistic manner. It does no good to take great care of the engine if the dangerously worn-out tires remain on the car. Maintaining overall health – physical, mental, emotional, intellectual, social, and spiritual – is critical. As opposed to the person who finally changes her diet after the first heart attack, we can save ourselves all sorts of trouble by living better and healthier each day. A good friend, Christopher Jones, tells people that the "today you" needs to benefit the "tomorrow you." What he means is that our daily actions ought to also be in our long-term best interests. While avoiding exercise as a young person might not cause devastating immediate consequences, the failure to develop that habit can lead to serious problems in adulthood.

Research has shown that laughter actually produces physiological benefits (and patients with cancer actually get better faster with more hugs), so we'd be wise to have fun along the way. Every day, I encounter crazy things that could be frustrating, but I work diligently to find reasons to laugh and keep these situations from stressing me out. Think of something really funny right now (such as the fact that the packet of silica gel inside the box for the pair of shoes you bought contains the words "Do not eat" on it – did anyone really expect a surprise snack?). Laugh. No, really allow yourself to laugh. Again, people who regularly laugh and laugh hard actually extend their lives! Even while passionately pursuing our goals, we need to make and take time to relax and celebrate life. If we are constantly on the go, we'll eventually run out of steam. That's why the culture in many countries encourages an afternoon break ("siesta") so that workers can charge back up for greater productivity.

Referring back to the "Paris in the the Spring" example, I feel that a critical component of this book involves helping readers to look at their lives and their thought processes from a whole different angle. This new perspective can allow individuals to recognize how certain practices might be unknowingly creating harm. In some ways, I consider myself to be a kind of "personal carbon monoxide detector," sounding the alarm to alert you to the presence of poisonous matter. Being a silent and odorless gas, the deadly carbon monoxide is difficult to detect. Along the same lines, some of our daily habits may be slowly but surely killing the spirit, without us even being aware of the problem. Awareness of these self-destructive processes can lead to change and assist in the overall goal of enhancing ownership.

A prime example of a subtle but dangerous practice for many people is the common excuse that "I forgot." I'm sure that many readers have found themselves in situations where they "forgot" to pay a bill or attend an event or contact a friend. Let me provide an entirely different interpretation here – since, in my opinion, the issue is actually not about forgetfulness per se. By saying we "forgot," the assumption is that the matter simply slipped out of our minds and that our behavior was completely unintentional. Wrong. We allow certain things to drift out of our consciousness if they are not deemed a priority. Thus, we usually don't really forget – we choose to allow ourselves the possibility of forgetting about it.

Let's be real here. No serious athlete has ever "forgotten" about a game, but that same individual might state that she "forgot" to complete an assignment for class. If it were important to her, she would have been certain to do whatever it took – from writing it down in an important place to asking others to remind her – to get it done. Thus, claiming forgetfulness allows us a passive excuse and reinforces the idea in our minds that it just might happen again without any power on our parts to change this reality. To me, that's problematic thinking. Reframing the statement by acknowledging how we allowed ourselves to forget grants us autonomy and the responsibility to do something differently in the future.

Similarly, I am amazed at how many people assert that they "don't have time" to complete even the simplest of tasks such as calling up a friend to say hello. If it's of value to you, then you make the time. I have often shown my classes a video of a family with eight children that incorporates business principles to ensure a harmonious home. By collaborating to work out a weekly family schedule, everybody's needs are met – and the whole group identifies a common timeslot to save in order to get together on a regular basis for dinner. Amazingly enough, many students reject the concept and assume that it's "impossible" to apply this time management model to their own families. For instance, the notion of a daily family meal is dismissed because "things come up." My response is that if every member knows that certain times are set aside for the family, few things just "come up" (or are allowed) to tamper with the program.

I remember hearing a story about a speaker who filled a gallon jar to the brim with huge rocks and asked audience if the jar were indeed full. The crowd responded yes. He then proceeded to pull out a cup of gravel and poured it inside the jar, with the little stones finding space between the big rocks. Once again, he asked the audience, "Is the jar full?" When they replied "probably not," he grabbed a bag of sand and poured it in. He asked about the jar being full now, and the participants in this mini-experiment shouted out "No!"

So, what's the point of this example? You might be tempted to state that it illustrates how we can always fit more into our lives, and indeed, there's truth to that idea. However, I see the bigger issue being that we need to take care of the "big rocks" first in life (family, health, financial well being, etc.). Too often, we get caught up in the little details and lose sight of what's really important to us. Not only is it essential to focus on and prioritize the "big rocks" to maximize our happiness, but by doing so, we can find time and place for the smaller things that often emerge. Think about it: if the sand and gravel were placed in the jar first, there wouldn't be enough room to put in all the big rocks.

How might the big and little rock concept be helpful for you?

_____

_____

_____

_____

As a closing example, my grandmother who passed away during the course of writing this book embodied many of the principles espoused in this chapter. While happily working alongside her husband for years in a business they built together, she truly loved raising her children and interacting with her grandchildren, tending to her garden, playing bridge with her friends, and pursuing various other hobbies. Even in her 89th year, while the doctors predicted that she would pass away within a few weeks, my grandmother resolved to stay alive until the following year to witness the Bar Mitzvah of her great-grandchild. Cancer may have ravaged her insides, Alzheimer's may have started to affect her brain – but her soul persevered, allowing her to hold out for 8 months in order to be able to experience the event in style. Thus, every day, you have the opportunity to take full ownership of your life, your emotions, your actions, your relationships, and ultimately, your future. Begin today. If so, you'll improve the quantity and quality of years lived.

Here's another fill in the blank for you: In order to take complete control of my life and destiny, I pledge to:

_____

_____

_____

_____

_____

_____

_____

_____

_____

_____

_____

_____

_____

Things I learned or thought about when reading this chapter:

_____

_____

_____

_____

_____

_____

_____

_____

_____

_____

_____

_____

CHAPTER FOUR

UNDERSTANDING
WE'RE DIFFERENT... AND WE'RE ALL THE SAME!

During a sabbatical in South Africa, I encountered a powerful phenomenon that reminded me of the impact of our beliefs. Since most people in my social network there did not own cars, I frequently ended up providing rides around town and enjoyed the chance to share experiences and discover cultural differences. It became common practice for visitors who spotted some food in the car to start consuming it without saying a word. In one instance, at a private function in the township organized in my honor, a young man I had not even met took some meat directly from my plate and started eating it.

I must admit that I initially found myself irritated by this behavior. Simply put, my American upbringing had taught me about individual rights and to assume that people should ask before taking. As a diversity consultant, I knew better and did assume that it was a cultural issue, but still, I felt a little bit uneasy about it all.

I mentioned the situation to a South African student with whom I had developed a strong relationship. After a hearty laugh, he expressed that, in his culture, "everything is shared... what's mine is yours and what's yours is mine." In contrast with

Western individualism, the concept of "ubuntu" ("brotherhood") leads members of the Xhosa tribal culture to embrace a sense of collective kinship. Think about it — you don't have to ask your mother for permission to get some juice when you're visiting her home. You just go to the fridge and indulge yourself. Well, this same sense of community operates within many tribes of South Africa. Indeed, no word for "stranger" even exists in any of the indigenous languages, symbolically prompting individuals to avoid seeing others as outsiders.

I had wrongly assumed that the notions of "private property" and "asking first" were universal ideas. But clearly, they're not. As Francesca Farr, a social worker quoted in the incredible book *The Spirit Catches You and You Fall Down* proclaims, "Our view of reality is only a view - not reality itself." We see the world from our own unique perspectives, and we must not presuppose that everybody sees it all as we do. As an example, think about the last argument you had with someone. I'm sure that both parties viewed the same situation in different ways. Yet, you were probably absolutely convinced that your interpretation was 100% correct - and so did the other person! Similarly, just because we have a particular way of doing things doesn't mean that it's inherently right.

This chapter is devoted to promoting greater cultural understanding, and since the world is becoming a global village (after all, salsa now outsells ketchup in the USA), it is critical that we learn to better understand ourselves and one another. Based on our unique and special cultures, we are very different - and this fact is worth celebrating. Knowing who we are and the richness of our backgrounds allows us to not only be proud of ourselves and our ancestors, but also to appreciate why others find such meaning in their cultures as well.

Yet, pride in oneself ought not yield an anti-other sentiment. In the melting-pot myth, we all blend into one homogenous mixture that denies our differences and advocates complete assimilation. I prefer the metaphor of the salad bowl, in which we acknowledge and encourage our varied cultural heritages while still identifying the value in coming together and finding unity through diversity. Celebrating our cultures has such incredible value – for example, research has consistently demonstrated that, in general, students who are fully bilingual are more cognitively developed than those speaking only one language.

As opposed to what I call the traditional "3Fs" approach to diversity – food, festivals, and famous people – I prefer to go far deeper into the realm of belief systems as evidence of our differences. Culture is "who we are and whose we are" – or as Herbert Gans writes, it's "the stories we tell ourselves about ourselves." It shapes every aspect of our lives and has a profound impact on how we experience the world and see our role in it. Culture does not simply refer to habits based on our ethnic group alone, but it also can be applied to the overall worldview of any social collective. If you belong to a church choir or a softball team, you know quite well how a series of expectations and customs applies to participants.

I contend that, when it comes to culture, we're different... and we're the same. We're different when it comes to gender. On double-dates, if one woman heads to the restroom, the other often joins her. Men rarely ask one another for assistance in that regard. While meant to be humorous, the example also points out some significant cultural differences – that, at least in this country, women are generally raised to be interdependent, while men are taught to be independent. On a serious note, because we tell males from an early age that "big boys don't cry," maybe that's why men have a much higher rate of violence, suicide, and substance abuse, because they turn to less productive means to deal with their pain and anger.

We're different when it comes to race and ethnicity. In East Indian culture, people are encouraged to eat with their right hands. Russian friends have told me that they are very uncomfortable with the constant smiling of Americans, whose actions would be perceived in their country as an indication of being stupid or sinister. Most of my African-American students report not being able to even imagine Thanksgiving dinner without homemade macaroni and cheese, yet most individuals of other backgrounds would be totally surprised by this tradition. OK, some of these examples might not seem profound, but they do speak to the fact that we often occupy different cultural worlds.

We're different when it comes to a whole host of other characteristics such as age (older folks tend to be far less comfortable with sharing personal details) and geographical location (Southern parents are more likely to require their children to say "sir" and "ma'am"). After speaking at a particular college, one professor mailed me copies of the papers that students had written about my presentation. One woman stated that she enjoyed the session, but that my style "reminded her of a Baptist preacher... [and] as Lutherans, we tend to be more reserved and I like it that way." The key is to celebrate our own styles while still respecting others who have divergent approaches to life.

Think of a cultural group that is important to you personally. For example, if I asked you, what are you – how would you respond? (You're actively involved in a wide variety of cultures, based on ethnicity, social clubs, religious affiliation, etc.) You might most proudly claim membership in Puerto Rican culture, hip-hop culture, school wrestling team culture, Lions Club culture, and so on. Why does it feel so special to belong to that cultural group? How does membership shape the way in which you view the world? How you participate in your family? How you express emotions? (It might seem odd that a supposedly "personal" issue such as emotions would have cultural components, but many of us learned lessons from our cultures about what emotions are appropriate to reveal, under what conditions, with whom, etc.) By being cognizant of how our cultures profoundly influence our thoughts and actions, we're in a better position to understand others and avoid making judgments that could lead us to disrespect those who do things differently than we do.

As an example, in mainstream American culture, showing respect to elders requires looking them in the eyes. Making direct eye contact is considered to be a critical social norm, indicating honesty and integrity. Yet, in most Asian cultures, one demonstrates full respect for older persons by looking down. Imagine the conflicts that have emerged in some classrooms when teachers failed to understand these cultural codes.

Just like we have blindspots when we're driving, I believe that we miss out on noticing many of these differences because of our cultural blindspots. We're so used to viewing life from our own perspective that it's difficult to see outside the box; indeed, a fish doesn't know it's wet until getting out of the water. Thus, we need to turn our heads a little bit and check out the world from new perspectives. As Stephen Covey writes, "Only by opening our mind to the possibility that we're not seeing everything will we be able to see what we're missing." Nobody could be reasonably expected to know all the practices of every group - but we can expect ourselves to be open to learning and to engage in behaviors that welcome others and create more inclusive spaces around us.

To illustrate these ideas, I'll ask you to take your index finger and place it about two inches in front of your nose. Now, alternate opening and closing your left and right eyes (go back and forth, with one eye open at a time). What happened? Did the finger move? Well, physically it didn't move, but your perspective did. Having two eyes provides us with depth perception, and we can't drive well without it. Similarly, it's helpful for us to have more depth in our understanding of the world - and we need multiple points of view to make that happen.

In a workshop conducted for future teachers, I asked participants to pair up and share views on controversial issues. As one woman revealed in the subsequent large-group discussion, she interacted with a man who identified with the Confederate flag - not for its racist heritage, but in his words, for "having pride in the Southern culture and way of life." While both she and I might find the flag's existence distasteful because of its symbolic meaning to certain groups, we both came to know a new perspective and therefore could avoid automatically viewing the man as a racist. Appreciating difference doesn't mean that we have to agree with ideas that are totally different from ours, but rather, that we ought to strive to understand and respect others. Indeed, we ought to seek first to understand, then to be understood – especially since if we are encouraging others to adopt a more open-minded position, we ought to model that behavior first by being willing to hear their point of view.

Listening and valuing others is a proactive process requiring time and emotional effort. I remember a student telling me about how his mother had essentially forbid him to continue an interracial relationship that he had established. Since he loved his girlfriend a great deal, he was extremely hurt by his mother's comments. Part of the problem for him was the concern that his mother apparently held racist beliefs, and in addition to planning to stay with the girlfriend, he intended to sever ties with his mom.

But, as we discussed the matter further, he discovered a possible alternate interpretation to the situation. Mom was a relatively recent immigrant to the country who held strong links to the culture as a source of pride, identity, and community connection. As he pondered the issue, he realized that she wasn't "against" other racial groups – just that she had feared how her only child would abandon their culture and that the family traditions would die out. Thus, it "made sense" that she might react negatively at first. Once he made the decision to sit down and really talk with his mom – letting her know how much he valued the culture and would preserve it – they grew closer together, with mom subsequently supporting the relationship.

However, while endeavoring to become more aware of our differences, we need to know that we're also all the same. We all want and deserve to be treated with dignity, to have freedom to be ourselves, to be loved. Therefore, we don't have the right to assume that others who don't play along with our belief systems are beneath us. The idea of denying equal rights to others because they are different is just flat-out wrong. Unless you'd like some other group to dominate you and impose its beliefs, avoid doing the same to others.

I recently read an essay by a leading politician in which he articulated a powerful point about faith. As a devout Christian, he celebrated the ways in which a spiritual foundation shaped his life and has served as the impetus for the inspired efforts of many great leaders and social activists. However, he cautioned fellow legislators and everyday citizens to see religion as a personal matter and not something to be forced upon others or used as a tool for denying human rights and dignity.

In my work on cultural competence, I contend that the most critical first step for all of us is to confront ourselves and our own biases. It's so easy for us to blame the noticeably prejudiced people while ignorantly and dangerously assuming our own innocence. Like it or not, we live in a society that is full of prejudice – and you can't swim in polluted waters and not have some of the poison stick to you.

Let's take an example. Pretend that you have 5-year-old twins, a boy and a girl. While on a trip to the local toy store, Little Maria pleasantly asks for a particular item as a present for her upcoming birthday – it's a basketball. Would you buy it? Well, about 95% of people in my workshops and classes seem to support the purchase of the ball.

Now, imagine that, after hearing the gleeful sounds of his sister receiving her desired gift, Little Jonathan approaches to provide his request. He wants a Baby-Boo-Boo, a life-like doll. Do you buy it? Most respondents say no. What does all this tell us? Clearly, we are very comfortable with expanding the world to girls and encouraging them to express themselves as they please. However, by denying him the doll, we seem to be letting boys know that a very narrow range of behavior is expected from them. It's sadly ironic that we complain a great deal in our society about men who abandon their children, yet we tell them early on that taking care of a baby is "for girls." Interestingly enough, most folks would buy Jonathan a GI Joe – a "doll" called an action figure to make it masculine enough to purchase. Basically, we're OK teaching boys about war but scared to encourage them to develop caring attributes. We all have biases.

Sometimes, we're not even aware of how pervasive and powerful these biases can be. In a study from a few years ago, researchers from the University of Chicago and MIT sent out resumes responding to jobs listed in the newspaper. One set of resumes carried "White-sounding" names, with the other ones having names that people typically associated with African-Americans. Besides the names, the resumes were the exact same. In the end, the White names received 50% more calls for interviews. I don't believe that most hiring personnel actively and intentionally discriminate against people of color, but something deep down triggers a negative reaction. They don't even recognize it, but it's there. Most right-handed students do not even realize that the desks in the classroom are designed for them, but every lefty notices the fact that they have to turn their bodies uncomfortably to be able to use the surface for writing.

Consider the following story. A man is driving late at night with his son, when the car inexplicably skids out of control and crashes into a tree. The father dies instantly, and the son who remains in critical condition is rushed to the hospital. In the emergency room, the doctor walks in, looks at the young man, and responds, "I cannot operate on him... he's my son." How do you explain what's happened? (Think before continuing to read.)

Well, here's the deal. No, it's not the father's stepson or anything like that. The doctor is the young man's mother! It's fascinating and scary that so many intelligent people somehow do not figure it out, and thus, this example demonstrates how our biases can creep in and influence our perceptions of reality.

True enough, going back to the "Paris in the the Spring" example from Chapter 1, just because you don't see it doesn't mean it's not there. Hopefully, we can all become more aware of the words and actions that might create discomfort for others, and instead of calling people "overly sensitive" for being offended, we can acknowledge their feelings and adjust accordingly. By walking a mile in someone else's shoes, we can discover so much about how others may not always receive the same treatment as we do. It's not about "political correctness" – but rather, about correctness. We all deserve to be treated with respect and dignity, and that's correct behavior.

Ultimately, I would hope that every one of us can be committed to fighting for the equality of all people. To be honest, if we're not engaged in the struggle, we're allowing oppressive conditions to persist. Many people believe that just because they do not say "bad" things about various groups, they are somehow absolved from responsibility to do something. Wrong. Removing discrimination from our society necessitates more active work to build greater opportunity for all people. The Civil Rights Movement didn't just happen. Rather, the struggle emerged as a result of the dedicated efforts of millions of individuals from all across the social spectrum – and it served as a source of spiritual motivation and tactical inspiration for a myriad of social movements that followed.

Furthermore, as Sir Edmund Burke once proclaimed, "All evil needs to flourish is for good people to remain silent." I am more disturbed by those who remain silent when hearing offensive comments than by the person who actually made the remark. That ignorant individual often doesn't know any better – but we do. Even if it's not "our group" being slandered, we ought to feel compelled to speak up and defend humanity. If we expect others to "have our backs," it's incumbent upon us to support other groups as they endeavor to achieve equality. As Senator Barack Obama stated after the institutional failure in the response to Hurricane Katrina, "Passive indifference is as bad as active malice." Charity is also no substitute for justice.

Here's a relevant analogy to consider: When starting an automatic vehicle, if you put the gear in "Drive," the car begins to roll. You don't have to press the gas. Similarly, even if we as individuals are not actively engaging in discriminatory practices, the car of societal inequality rolls on. We need to put the foot on the brake and work towards stopping the rampant levels of sexism, racism, homophobia/heterosexism, and the other "isms" that exist in the first place. We need to be, as Gandhi said, "the example that we wish to see in the world." In the words of the famed Archbishop Desmond Tutu, "If you are neutral in situations of injustice, you have chosen the side of the oppressor. If an elephant has his foot on the tail of a mouse and you say that you are neutral, the mouse will not appreciate your neutrality."

While our nation is wrapped up in worrying about being hurt by terrorists from outside, I worry as much about the internal micro-terrorism we all seem to commit daily. Whenever we criticize or condemn someone for being different, we engage in a form of terrorism. Whenever we attempt to destroy someone's dreams or their spirit, we're terrorists. Whenever we play victim to our fears and crush our own hopes, it's terrorism. True "homeland security" means looking in our mirrors and making the home around us a safe and productive one for ourselves and others. May we all rally our own personal troops for the safety and freedom of everyone.

We can make a difference by using our knowledge, passion, and energy to embrace others. The famed anthropologist Margaret

Mead provided us with a powerful line about our potential for generating transformation: "Never doubt that a small group of thoughtful, committed citizens can change the world. Indeed, it's the only thing that ever has." Even if just the people reading this book dedicated themselves to making personal changes, to boldly reaching out to others, to getting involved in some movement for positive change... we'd see incredible progress. There are plenty of children in our local communities who need someone to read with them, and so many older citizens who spend their final days alone in a facility. Get involved. With 168 hours in a week, I'm convinced that we can all find at least one hour to give to others and society as a whole.

In my opinion, we are responsible for building a better world and to providing assistance wherever possible. It is heartening to read that volunteerism is on the rise among young people and that many educators are requiring their students to complete some type of service project to learn and to give back. As the old saying goes, "To whom much is given, much is required." Indeed, if you feel that this book has been beneficial, then it is incumbent upon you to "pay it forward" by educating or inspiring someone else. In the words of Amelia Earhart, "Some of us have great runways already built for us. If you have one, take off! But if you don't have one, realize it is your responsibility to grab a shovel and build one for yourself and for those who will follow after you."

Multiculturalism isn't just something that you engage in sporadically when attending a workshop or a local cultural festival. To the contrary, true commitment to its principles requires making the inclusive way of life and the dedication to social justice a complete part of our daily practice. As an educator, you don't simply "add on" a section to your course, but rather, infuse the spirit into your entire curriculum and teaching approach. As a parent, it is critical that your children consistently receive direct exposure and hear positive messages about various social groups in order to counterbalance what may be erroneous and hostile images being presented to them by others. Diversity is not to be "managed" (as if it's a negative thing) nor is it simply about "tolerance" (people should be respected and understood, not merely tolerated) – it's a wonderful element in our society that should be cherished.

When I first began my work with young people in inner-city Chicago, I had internalized negative impressions about hip-hop culture and informed my students that any cassette tapes (yes, that's what we had back in the day!) with "bad" language that they played in my car would be immediately confiscated and thrown out the window. I felt convinced that my moral stance would teach a positive lesson, yet it demonstrated cultural ignorance and arrogance. One day, a student simply asked, "Before judging it all, would you just really listen to some of it?" Not only did the subsequent process of fully encountering the music show my students that I cared about their world, but it helped me to gain a new appreciation of the potential power of hip-hop culture and its meaning to today's youth. It brought us closer together... and, in the end, I have become somewhat of an expert on hip-hop who is frequently asked to lecture on the topic around the country! Being open to others builds relationships and offers us chances to grow as well.

Finally, I am reminded of a story that I heard years ago about a young girl walking on an ocean beach. As Samantha kicked up sand, she found a buried starfish that had begun to die. Immediately concerned about its welfare, the girl placed the starfish back into the water. But, she soon discovered countless starfish in a similar predicament up ahead on the beach. Samantha moved into high gear and started a heroic rescue effort. Upon seeing this behavior, the girl's brother started to laugh and tease her: "There are thousands of starfish up on this beach, so there's no way that you can save them all." Undeterred by his remarks, the girl picked up a starfish, and before saving it by hurling it into the water, she proudly proclaimed to her brother, "True – but I made a difference for this one!"

As famed scholar Cornel West has written, "None of us alone can save the world. But each of us can make a positive difference if we commit ourselves to do so." In a world often consumed by inhumane treatment, it is so important to reach out to others and break the cycle of hatred and inequality. We can, and indeed we must, do better to ensure that every person feels respected and provided with full equal opportunity for success.

Another set of fill-in-the-blanks for your benefit: Being honest with myself, I recognize that I hold some biases that need to be addressed – what are they and how can I remove them?

_____

_____

_____

_____

_____

_____

_____

_____

_____

_____

_____

_____

When it comes to getting involved in personal and social change to bring about inclusion and equity, I pledge to:

_____

_____

_____

_____

_____

_____

_____

_____

_____

_____

_____

_____

Things I learned or thought about when reading this chapter:

_____

_____

_____

_____

_____

_____

_____

_____

_____

_____

_____

C H A P T E R   F I V E

TEAMWORK
NONE OF US IS AS SMART OR PRODUCTIVE AS ALL OF US!

I f you have ever carefully watched geese in flight, you might have noticed that they typically travel in "V" formation. First of all, the geese share roles and practice communal responsibility. When the lead goose gets tired, it rotates positions with another. That way, no goose burns out, and every single one has the chance to take the front position. If one goose becomes sick or wounded so that it falls out of formation, two others follow it down and lend help. Furthermore, the geese in the back of the flock actually produce the honking sounds you hear, with the intent of encouraging the ones towards the front to maintain their speed.

But most importantly, flying in the "V" that resembles wings on an airplane provides 71 percent greater wind speed for the geese, propelling the entire flock towards its destination more quickly and easily. Think about it. Instead of flying alone, the goose that joins the flock but continues to fly with the same amount of energy actually goes considerably faster. None of us is as smart or productive as all of us – and if we're as wise as the geese, we'd pull together and accomplish more. As stated earlier in the book, it's not always a case of working "harder" but working smarter in our lives.

Something magical happens when a group coalesces and functions well together. You can probably think of some group that you participated in that was so enjoyable. Perhaps it was a sports team or a special social club. When everyone felt united, the performance level increased. You wanted to do well, and the bonds of trust between members reinforced this commitment. Studies have shown that groups of people pulling together on a rope in a game of tug-o-war generate more force than the sum of all their individual previous efforts. Working together inspires them to give and produce a little bit extra. As an African proverb states, "I am because we are, and we are because I am."

Yet, current studies indicate that we are growing more isolated in our society and spend far less time in collective engagement. I have even noticed how new homes built in the South where I live are absent of the front porches that typified a spirit of neighborly interaction, instead replaced by private back decks. We can be more productive - and life is so much richer - when immersing ourselves with others in healthy social exchange.

To accomplish our goals, we may need a little support from different people. Too many individuals (particularly males) have a problem asking for help, believing somehow that it is an indication of "weakness." Have you ever been in a car with one of those folks who would rather drive around lost for hours than ask for directions? As a wise person once stated, "Pride is the only poison that will kill you if you don't swallow it." To me, it seems to be incredibly weak to have a problem and refuse to seek assistance. I wonder, why be so afraid to address the issue? Isn't it weak to give in to those insecurities and remain in a bad situation? It is a definite sign of strength to know when something is wrong and to be "man" or "woman" enough to work towards getting better. We don't hesitate to go see a doctor to heal a broken arm, so why not do the same with a broken heart, mind, or spirit?

To illustrate this point, I often tell the story about how I made a pledge during my teenage years to never vomit again. I hated the feeling and thought that I could control my body forever. Now, since I have never been drunk, that pledge seemed like a relatively easy thing to accomplish. Well, one day, after a particularly horrible meal, I discovered the wonderful world of food poisoning. For hours, I remained diligent in this quest to stay vomit-free, but eventually realized that the toxins just needed to get out of my system. And indeed, upon throwing up, I felt so much better. I needed to let go and let it all go. Sometimes, we hesitate to open up to others when we're going through difficult times, and instead, we remain burdened by our emotions. Just letting it go and getting it off our chests can lighten the load and help us to see the issues from a different point of view. I remember so many instances when simply talking about a concern allowed me to better understand the situation, even without any feedback from the listener.

Since none of us is as smart or productive as all of us, the presence and insights of others can assist us in preparing to make more informed decisions. It's an interesting reality that almost no one who is ticklish can tickle themselves - someone else is "needed" to do the job. Similarly speaking, there are some things that we may not be capable of doing by ourselves, so take the chance to reach out and accept support. According to former Supreme Court Justice Sandra Day O'Connor, "We don't accomplish anything in this world alone... and whatever happens is the result of the whole tapestry of one's life and all the weavings of individual threads from one to another that creates something."

In his theories regarding brain-based learning, Eric Jensen discusses how we learn far more when we encounter new information in a variety of ways. Thus, just hearing a lecture or only knowing one perspective has less value than incorporating a number of different strategies and gaining many people's points of view. Jensen argues that only using one approach ends up literally making our brains shrink in size. Exercising our brains on a wide range of "intelligence machines" through engagement with others helps them to grow and stay alert.

If we want to achieve the benefits of synergy, we must endeavor to treat others well. On general principle, we ought to interact with everyone in humane ways – but as an added bonus, it's important to recognize how all interactions can have profoundly positive or negative consequences for us. When I was younger, I made some mistakes and ended up alienating people who could have been valuable resources. I also know that some of my positive connections with young people have had a truly meaningful impact on their lives, as they have reported years later. The negative encounters tend to have more profound implications, as research has indicated that the typical customer having a good experience tells five people, but the individual with the bad experience shares the story with fifteen others.

First, it is valuable for all readers to self-reflectively assess their typical modes of emotional expression. What seems to trigger sadness or anger, and how can you proactively recognize when it's about to happen so that you can find a solution? What seems to calm you down, establish focus, and achieve joy – deep breaths, self-talk, exercise, or something else? You can feel without always having to react negatively – and true power is not control over others, but rather, over our own emotional affairs. If you don't like some of the patterns you've noticed, then you can change them! As Jonatan Martensson states, "Feelings are much like waves. We can't stop them from coming, but we can choose which ones to surf."

I once heard a preacher talk about the difference between heaven and hell. She said that hell was like the biggest buffet with all the food we absolutely love – but individuals there lacked the elbow or hip joints needed to bring the feast to their mouths. That's frustrating. Heaven, on the other hand, involves the exact same buffet and same physical condition. However, in this situation, people sit across from one another and feed each other. Can you imagine what kind of world we could create if we would take the time to spiritually feed one another, to really listen to and support each other? If we would strive to reach out and offer help, even when we're not being asked or even if it's not in our job description?

Every reader has a series of relationships to maintain, all of which require emotional energy. Thus, it is critical to pay more attention to how we handle emotions in our interactions with significant others. If you're frustrated at work and bring it home, you might strain the connections between you and your family members or with a romantic partner. Remember, it's not your mom's fault that your biology professor gave the class a killer test. At the same time, losing your temper with co-workers because "my girlfriend is acting crazy" isn't fair to them either. Thus, it's critical to monitor your emotions and proactively work to find ways to keep everything balanced. While it may seem overwhelming to manage these relationships, it's possible. It just takes what scholar Daniel Goleman calls "emotional intelligence," and I'd like to share some tips for sharpening your skills in this area.

Let's focus the discussion now on the issue of conflict resolution. Too often, we view conflict as an inherently bad thing or as simply an opportunity to beat somebody (physically or mentally). Conflict is inevitable in life, but it can actually produce valuable results when handled appropriately, as individuals have a chance to address lingering concerns and finally find solutions. You can probably recall a time when arguing with a friend eventually ended up bringing you closer together. By putting everything on the proverbial table and taking the risk of being fully honest, the process of working through the situation ended up enhancing bonds of trust. Relationship research has consistently shown that the best predictor of long-term success is the ability of the couple to "fight well."

So, recall a recent disagreement with someone else. How did you handle it? If you "went postal" on them, did it really help?

Were you committed to proving yourself right and them wrong? They probably did the same thing, with the situation spiraling downhill into a mess.

Hopefully, you can approach most situations with a "win-win" mentality: "I may be angry, but how can we both leave here with a better understanding and less hostility?" Most folks in American culture want to be the victor, but if that's your goal, watch out - they'll be coming for you the next time! A "win over" today can actually end up becoming a major loss in the long run.

Even when dealing with difficult people, it's possible to make the situation better. Sometimes, the trick is to identify something meaningful that you share in common with him/her - and once that connection has been established, you'll be amazed at how much more likely a positive outcome can be. It is part of the human condition to desire to belong, to be understood, to find common ground.

I'd like to share with you a powerful line that can get you out of some bad situations. When confronted by a mean manager or a ticked-off tyrannical teacher, try calmly asking, "What would you like me to do?" It's amazing how the other person's tone changes quickly, because you've put the emphasis on them and forced them to think rather than just emotionally go off on you. Your willingness to move the conversation to the solutions phase often produces better results.

Also, before bringing criticism to others, think carefully about the best way to approach the situation. Indeed, would you want someone to attack you in front of others or to use language that is intentionally hurtful? It often helps to consider the context, as most people prefer to be approached in private and when they are prepared to engage in a discussion. Just because you need to talk doesn't mean that it's the ideal time for them.

I once worked with a supervisor who elected to chastise staff members in e-mails sent to the entire department. The technique was clearly intended to embarrass and alienate the individual while threatening others with possible public ridicule for future transgressions. Any feelings of unity and trust quickly went out the window.

We have the right to raise concerns but not to abuse others. The words we use also have a powerful impact on the likelihood of success. As you know, what you say is often not nearly as important as how you say it. Many people find the following phrase (fill in the blanks accordingly) to be helpful in crafting a meaningful message that will get your feelings out and enable you to be heard:

"I feel _____ when you _____.

I'd like for you/us to _____."

By using "I" messages, your words are more likely to be listened to by the other person. When someone starts a conversation with us by saying, "You always (fill-in-the-criticism)," we tend to get defensive and desire to fight back. You may want to go on the offensive when you're addressing a concern that deeply disturbs you, but is it really going to be as productive?

I have also devised a systematic way to handle conflicts, entitled the CLEAR method. Sure, in the heat of the moment, it may not be entirely feasible to remember all of the following steps in order – but the goal is for you to integrate the basic principles into your overall approach.

Calm down and think about the situation.

Before confronting someone, relax and determine if it's necessary to do something. Perhaps you might want to remember the old saying, "Don't sweat the small stuff." Ask yourself, "Why am I upset, and what is the best way to handle this situation?"

Look at the issue from both sides.

It is valuable to understand why the other person might be acting or feeling that way. It's possible that difficult life experiences at the moment may lead them to be responding in a manner that is not typical for them. Also, remember that there are three sides to every story – yours, theirs, and the truth. Keep in mind that your opinion or interpretation might not always be accurate.

Express your feelings respectfully.

Using "I" messages, let the other person know how you feel without attacking or placing blame. Be specific about what led you to feel this way and suggest ways for the situation to be resolved while encouraging their ideas as well.

Actively listen.

Allow the other person to tell his/her side of the story without interruption or argument. Do not simply wait to hear something that you can immediately criticize. Remember, your goal is not to hurt him/her but to resolve the conflict effectively. Watch your body language to ensure that you are paying full attention and showing respect.

Resolve the situation as best as possible.

If possible, find some way to work through the situation and move forward. Brainstorm ideas to proactively work towards not having the problem arise again. You may end up with a compromise, so be open to new ideas and possibilities. As relationship expert John Gottman claims, compromise is not giving in, but rather, a creative and evolving process of making something new that has never existed before. I like that idea. You're not being weak; you're being wise enough to produce an original solution that works best. Congratulations!

OK, it may seem odd to follow a formula for fighting fair. But, it can really work. I remember sharing this information with gang members in a special program, with one young man dismissing the possible utility of this approach in his neighborhood. Yet the following week, he returned to announce that he had implemented his own version of the technique and achieved success. Whatever works for you is great.

Finally, I wish to share thoughts on the power of forgiveness. All of us have been treated wrongly by others in life. Many readers have probably been deeply hurt by the troubling actions of people whom we trusted. I suggest that the act of forgiveness can be one of the most powerful and liberating practices possible. You might feel that you're "giving in" or "accepting" the troubling behavior if you forgive the other person. It's not about that. When we are genuinely able to forgive – and it doesn't have to be directed to the person, as we can silently forgive them or write a letter that's never mailed – we begin the process of healing for ourselves. Forgiveness is about releasing oneself from the bondage of pain and anger. What good does it do to stay mad at dad for your whole life? It certainly grants you a convenient excuse, but those negative feelings only serve to hold you back. Research is clear about the uplifting power of forgiveness.

Living and working together takes effort, but it yields amazing results. Ever notice that sometimes you can solve other people's problems but have difficulty putting that same plan into motion for yourself? We do need each other – for feedback, insight, motivation, love, support, encouragement, and challenge. Let's all put in the work to bring out the best in every single one of us.

It's fill-in-the-blank time: When it comes to living and working with others for greater benefit, I pledge to:

_____

_____

_____

_____

_____

_____

_____

_____

_____

_____

_____

We all have relationships that need repairing or people we need to forgive or ask forgiveness from. Use this space to process those ideas and maybe practice what you can say to those individuals.

_____

_____

_____

_____

_____

_____

_____

_____

_____

_____

_____

_____

Things I learned or thought about when reading this chapter:

_____

_____

_____

_____

_____

_____

_____

_____

_____

_____

FINAL THOUGHTS

It's All ABOUT You Now!

If you think about it, life is truly a precious gift to be treasured. On the night that each of us was conceived (I know we don't like to think about our parents having sex, but well, they did!), there were approximately 500 million sperm swimming around, each representing a different person. In fact, in the whole history of the world, there has only been one egg and one sperm - out of the trillions created — that could have possibly become you. And you were chosen. Yes, had another set of egg and sperm been selected, it might have had your name, but it would not have been you. Indeed, just by being born, we are chosen people. (Those 500-million-to-one odds make being conceived about 25 times harder than winning the Lotto jackpot in most states.) We must therefore cherish the gift of life that has been presented to us and live to the fullest. You've been placed here for a purpose - and hopefully, this book has helped you to identify that purpose and to realize your many talents, opportunities, and responsibilities.

In my presentations, I use a wonderful activity in which participants tie small strands of yarn on each other while giving out words of praise and hugs. Too often, we are so preoccupied by gossip and negativity that we fail to take the time to really let others know how much we admire and appreciate them. It's amazing how much saying something positive can mean to someone - and conversely, how devastating our attacks can truly be. Most of us know that one hurtful or helpful comment can literally turn a person's whole day or life around. Since, according to one study, successful couples tend to share with each other at least five positive things to every one criticism in order to maintain a healthy relationship, it would be helpful if we would all be more cognizant of how we speak to people and offer nicer words. I always watching large groups engage in this exercise, witnessing the smiles and tears of joy that permeate the room as people feel safe to express their feelings of appreciation. It's not just about us in life – hopefully, we can help one another to make life better for all.

After fifty years on the job, a housebuilder decided to hang up his hardhat and hammer to pursue a leisurely retirement. The boss, however, needed this man to construct one more house. He told the builder, "Look, the people who want this house built have an odd request. They want me to ask my best worker to do whatever he wants – to create any kind of house he wishes and to spend as much time and money as he pleases." While puzzled by this unique request, the man felt proud that he was viewed as the company's top builder and agreed to do the work. The boss handed the man a doorknob and informed him that the only requirement of the job was to place it on the front door.

A few hours later, the builder returned to the boss and claimed to be finished. He had taken the request literally and simply created a little outhouse with second-rate effort and materials. He knew that the same amount of pay would be provided if he worked half a day or half a year, so why bother with more work? The boss asked if he needed additional time, but the man handed him a note and replied, "Nope, I'm done – you can send my final check to the address on this piece of paper." Pleased with himself for easily snagging extra money with minimal effort, he walked away with a swagger.

The boss waited a few moments before calling out the builder's name. He quickly tossed a key at the man and looked him in the eye when telling him the news: "I was hoping to send the check to a different address. You see, this house was my gift to you." The builder could have created for himself the ultimate dream house. He didn't – and he ended up shortchanging himself. Similarly, if we don't give our all in life, we end up with the same feeling of disappointment and regret.

It might help to remember this story as you journey through life. You have the opportunity to build a beautiful home for yourself. You have the abilities to make incredible things happen for you. Will you take advantage of the powerful resources inside of you and around you to create the kind of house that you can be most proud of? Will you lay out a meaningful plan for success? Will you maintain ownership of the house and continue to seek out new home improvements that will allow you to enjoy it even more each day? Will you endeavor to build happiness within the home by ensuring that everyone who ventures inside it feels understood and respected? Will you share your gifts with others to ensure that they possess the tools needed to construct wonderful homes for themselves? I believe that you can and that you will. Indeed, the answer is now in your very capable hands!

Final fill-in-the-blanks: As a result of reading this book, I will:

_____

_____

_____

_____

_____

_____

Because:

_____

_____

_____

_____

_____

_____

Here are the most important ideas or lessons that I learned from reading this book:

_____

_____

_____

_____

_____

_____

_____

_____

_____

_____

_____

Notes: